INSTITUTE OF CLASSICAL ARCHITECTURE & ART
20 West 44th Street, Suite 310, New York, NY 10036
telephone (212) 730-9646 facsimile (212) 730-9649

WWW.CLASSICIST.ORG

EDITOR
Steven W. Semes

DESIGNER
Dyad Communications *design office*
Philadelphia, Pennsylvania

PUBLISHER
Henrika Dyck Taylor

PRINTER
Crystal World Printing
Manufactured in China

ISBN 978-0-9642601-5-8
ISSN 1076-2922

FRONT COVER
"In the Pantheon, Rome," watercolor on paper, 30" x 22", 2008, by Alexander Creswell.

BACK COVER
Verre Eglomisé Frieze Detail by Miriam Ellner, winner of the Arthur Ross Award for Artisanship, 2013. The "three graces" are gilded and etched in 22 karat gold leaf and surrounded by octagonal moon gold frames and overlapping palladium mechanical gears. Photograph by Wiley Kidd.

FRONT AND BACK END PAPERS
"The Rome of Alexander VII," graphite on paper, 39 ¾" x 66", 2013, by Daniel Heath.

SECTION OPENING IMAGES
PAGES 6-7: M. Piacentini and A. Guazzaroni, with the collaboration of V. Pardo, project for the National Stadium, Rome, 1910. Aerial perspective. (Archivio Storico Capitolino, Fondo Contratti, Atti Pubblici, 238, 7 dicembre 1911). PAGES 36-37: Academy of Classical Design. Students Allison Sexton and Olena Babak at work on paintings from plaster casts of antique statuary, 2013. Photograph courtesy of the Academy of Classical Design. PAGES 56-57: U.S. Federal Building and Courthouse, Tuscaloosa, Alabama. View of main entrance. Photograph by Timothy Hursley. PAGES 78-79: The "Sky Ceiling" of the Main Concourse, from *Grand Central Terminal: 100 Years of a New York Landmark* by the New York Transit Museum and Anthony W. Robins, Stewart, Tabori & Chang, 2012. Reproduced with permission. PAGES 92-93: Model of The Pantheon, Rome, in gypsum plaster with additional detail in white metal and etched brass, 22" x 18" x 15", by Timothy Richards, Bath, United Kingdom, winner of the Arthur Ross Award for Artisanship, 2013.

The generous contributions of individuals and institutions who provided images for publication, the invaluable assistance of the anonymous peer reviewers of the academic articles, and the resourceful participation by Gay Giordano, Kate Koza, Peter Spalding, and Nora Reilly are all gratefully acknowledged.

THE CLASSICIST

№11: 2014

THE CLASSICIST *is an annual peer-reviewed journal dedicated to the advancement of the core values of the Institute of Classical Architecture & Art by providing a venue for scholarship related to the classical tradition in architecture and the allied arts, a forum for current classical practice, and a source of information and inspiration for students, practitioners, teachers, patrons, and lovers of classical art and architecture.*

The Classicist at Large
REMEMBERING HENRY HOPE REED, JR. (1915–2013)

"*Yes, the road we take will eventually lead to Rome, where God, emperor and Man have been glorified. In that city which has been the end of all pilgrimages of architects and civic designers there is no fear to use any instrument in attaining the monumental effect, be it sculpture, mosaic, painting, gliding, gold, stucco, or the orders. It is not "honest" architecture, it is not "clean," it is not "hygienic," but it is magnificent, glorious, and soul-consoling. There we can see the majestic concept, the street or the flight of steps leading to the square surrounded by richly ornamented monuments, where the lamp of power was once rubbed and gave forth magnificence.*" [1]

These words, from one of the first published essays of Henry Hope Reed, are surely counter-cultural. Glory of what? Magnificence to what end? To speak longingly of glory in 1952 seemed little short of delusional, as it may still seem today. Wasn't the pursuit of glory what had led humanity into a series of catastrophic wars—seeking glory in the state, in a race, in a creed or church, in loyalty to King, Emperor, Duce, Party Secretary, or Führer? The world after 1945, it seemed, had to reject glory because it had been attached to unsuitable objects, just as an individual might reject love after finding that he or she had loved the wrong person. Henry Reed understood that, but he also knew that glory, like faith, hope, and love, was a fundamental human need that could not be denied simply because it had once been misdirected. But what, in an age of radical skepticism and unbelief, or worse, of consumerism and populist kitsch, could possibly inspire the kind of glory that shone out from all the great art and architecture of the past?

Henry did not believe the horrors of modern times had closed off the legitimate aims toward which the artist, or society in general, had historically aspired. We still have values worth celebrating in architecture, but they are no longer exclusive: What had been the property of tyrants, princes, or popes was now the heritage of everyone. The inspiration for glory would now come from the values of democracy, from civic virtue, from communities dedicated to social harmony, justice, and peace. The San Francisco Civic Center and City Hall by Arthur Brown, Jr., to which Henry dedicated a rousing peroration in his book, *The Golden City*, calling it "the best that American art has produced," could show us how. *There* was glory and magnificence; *there* was monumentality, but celebrating and inspiring the citizens of a beautiful, proud, and fiercely democratic city. Henry knew that this kind of grand, civic, classical architecture fulfilled a basic need and expressed a necessary hope, although retrieving it today would require a massive cultural regeneration. Undaunted, he was confident that it would come. "What people have done well once they can do again," he declared, in blissful disregard of the prevailing Hegelian notions of the cultural elite.

Henry's conception of architecture was essentially visual rather than theoretical, and urban rather than abstract. Curiously, he does not offer a neat definition of the classical in his books; rather, he presents classicism as the normative culture of Western building based on an ancient formal language whose principal means is the exaltation of the human figure and whose crowning purpose is the building of the beautiful and just city. The urban emphasis is essential because it is the city that gathers our aspirations and opens up the life of freedom; its physical setting should therefore be magnificent. The classical city is humane, welcoming, uplifting, and above all, pleasing. The modernist city, on the contrary, is formless and placeless. These two visions are contrasted in the opening chapter of *The Golden City*, in which Henry juxtaposed images of classical and modernist buildings, public spaces, monuments, and street furniture, to devastating effect. "Every generation of classical architecture has its own vision of perfection and its own Golden City," he declared, and his advocacy of the classical urban vision in the face of derision or indifference was nothing short of courageous.

Henry understood architecture, urbanism, and decorative art as a continuum ranging across scales, from the design of city streets and squares, parks, and neighborhoods, to buildings, monuments, fountains, flagpoles, and balustrades. All of these could speak to us of glory, even without being monumental in scale or character. A small park or square adorned with beds of flowers, a fountain, statuary, and handsome benches was as much a celebration of human values as New York's great Central Park, of which Henry served as Curator. When New Urbanists speak of pedestrian scale and a street's "walk score," they are, whether they admit it or not, heirs of the peripatetic urbanism Henry initiated in the 1950s with his New York walking tours. These didactic promenades demonstrated the contribution of architecture to making a street "walkable," irrespective of the calculations of the planners. And the principal source of visual interest in buildings, for Henry, was ornament.

Ornament was the common thread—one might say obsession—that drew his thought into a unity. Ornament and decoration were the true test of a genuine classical architecture. From the simple egg-and-dart to the flowing acanthus to the ennobled human figure, classical ornament gives life to buildings, affords a lively play of light and shade, introduces narrative and symbolic content, and facilitates the reading of scale. He railed against architects—even those classically trained—who fixated on abstract formal design to the exclusion of the ornament, which for him, lifted building into the realm of art. "What is more depressing," he would ask, "than a blank pediment?" Doubtless the unadorned walls and stark detailing of much contemporary classical design is due in part to the isolation in which architects are now trained, no longer sharing a curriculum with painters and sculptors, as they did in the old Beaux-Arts system. It likely also reflects lingering uncertainty about content and the legitimacy of glory. Despite these limitations, the great themes of the human condition are finding new narratives for our time in the ancient but ever-evolving language of classical ornament.

Even more than modernism, Henry's adversary was the dry theory and abstraction that diverted architecture from its primary mission as mother of the arts. It was from a cramped rationalism that modernism itself sprang. Late in his career, he began referring to modernist design as "anorexic architecture," a kind of visual malnourishment imposed in the name of arcane theory. The classical was the ever-present antithesis of this self-impoverishment, and every city and town in America offered some example worthy of study. Rising above them all was always Rome, a city built not on theory, but on beauty. In contrast with the intentional meaninglessness of contemporary art, Rome embodied enduring significance; instead of disposable construction, it offered as much permanence as human labor affords; and rather than being limited by the values of particular times or political orders, it transcended all of them to embody a perennial humanism. This, in the end, is what Henry meant by glory.

Henry's crusade accelerated in 1968 with his founding of Classical America together with a small band of like-minded pioneers. The organization's eponymous journal, its classes in drawing and design, the annual Arthur Ross Awards, and the publication of seminal texts like *The American Vignola* and *Letarouilly on Renaissance Rome* in the "Classical America Series in Art and Architecture" raised public awareness of the tradition and recognized contemporary contributions to it. Classical America offered training in the tradition when such instruction was available nowhere else. Outstanding among his own books were monographs on the New York Public Library, the Library of Congress Jefferson Building, and the United States Capitol: they are simply among the best textbooks on classical design ever produced. Beyond these achievements, he was an unflagging mentor and resource for dozens of aspiring classical architects, artists, craftsmen, and patrons, a role he continued after the conglomeration of Classical America and the Institute of Classical Architecture in 2002.

In view of his remarkable career, we can say that every volume of *The Classicist* has in some way been a tribute to Henry Hope Reed, but this volume is explicitly dedicated to his memory. We are not unmindful

that he was an exacting critic who never hesitated to point out errors or what he saw as lapses in taste here and there. Nevertheless, we offer this volume as a partial fulfillment of his prediction, over half a century ago, that the classical would return to contemporary practice in architecture and the allied arts, in public and private works. However much further we have yet to go to fulfill that goal, we can take considerable satisfaction in our progress so far. Henry, we could not have done it without you. —SWS

Figure 1 (above): Henry Hope Reed, Jr., at the Palazzo Mattei, Rome, circa 1950. Photograph reproduced with the permission of the Estate of Henry Hope Reed, Jr.

[1] Reed, Jr., Henry Hope, "Monumental Architecture, or the Art of Pleasing in Civic Design," *Perspecta*, 1, Summer 1952, p. 56. Reprinted with the permission of *Perspecta*, Yale School of Architecture.

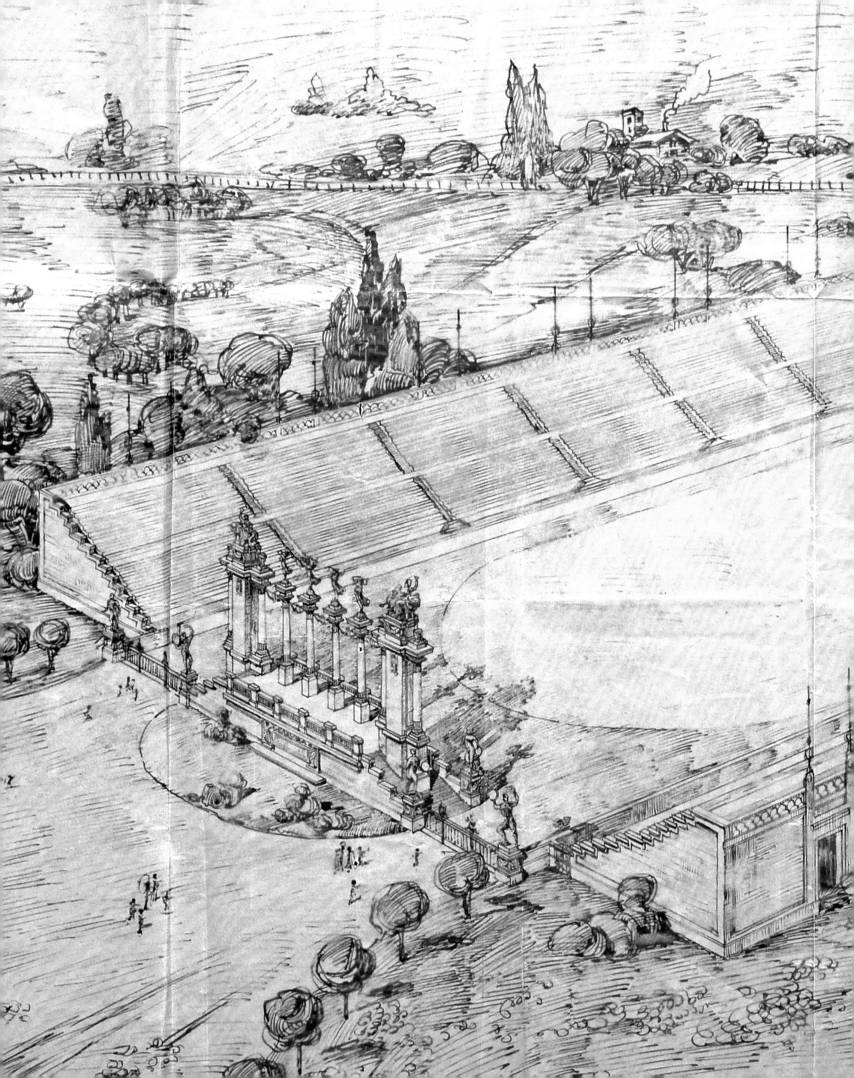

Essays

Ancient Taste Perfected by Modern Hands
THOMAS U. WALTER'S THEORY AND PRACTICE OF THE ORDERS

By Jhennifer A. Amundson, Ph.D.

A LIVING ARTISTIC TRADITION REQUIRES BOTH CANON AND INVENTION: THOMAS U. WALTER'S MOVEMENT FROM IMITATION TO EMULATION OF ANTIQUE PRECEDENT MIRRORS THE NINETEENTH-CENTURY CLASSICAL REVIVAL'S DEVELOPMENT FROM ANTIQUARIAN PRACTICE BASED ON PUBLISHED SOURCES TOWARD A MORE EXPRESSIVE USE OF THE ANCIENT LANGUAGE.

Although he practiced in several historic traditions throughout his lengthy career, Thomas U. Walter (1804-87) favored the language of classicism, especially for his most significant civic projects. Although a cursory familiarity with Girard College (Philadelphia, 1832-45) [FIGURE 1] and the United States Capitol (Washington, 1850-65) [FIGURE 2] illustrates his general interest in the Greco-Roman tradition, a closer analysis reveals a change in Walter's theoretical positions over the course of his career. This shift is especially visible in his handling of the orders, which evolved from a manner that might be termed archaeological—a careful, exacting reproduction of select precedents—to one that was more emulative—maintaining the spirit and character of the originals while rivaling them with modern innovations. Early in his career, Walter understood the orders to be inviolate; capricious additions and changes could only demean their purity and beauty. As Walter's theoretical understanding of classicism and its role as an architectural language matured during the first half of the nineteenth century, he increasingly explored its adaptability for new expressions.

FOUNDATIONS

During the 1820s in Philadelphia, Walter enjoyed opportunities for architectural education and training that were unusual in America until much later in the nineteenth century. As a pupil in the office of William Strickland, Walter observed and participated in the practice of

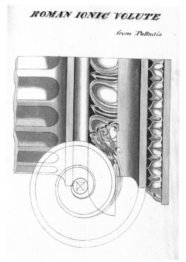

ROMAN IONIC VOLUTE

from Palladio

a prolific designer who clearly articulated his stylistic preferences. Strickland believed that ancient Greek architecture offered the best and most appropriate model to American builders because of its ability to express the roots of democracy and the spirit of republicanism; he encouraged his own pupils to think likewise. Strickland's ideas are preserved in lecture notes that he presented at the Franklin Institute, where Walter had enrolled as a student in 1824. These lectures focused on the Greek orders as the foundational elements for a fundamentally American architecture by virtue of their derivation, history, and aesthetic purity. Strickland presented key monuments, as described in famous folios, as models that modern architects should follow scrupulously to achieve the strength, beauty, proportion and symmetry that arose from the "permanent principles" and "laws of order" inherent in the Greek orders.[1] This was especially true in the canonical Athenian monuments, which Strickland affirmed as the models "educated men have in all ages agreed to admire." Their forms and proportions required careful attention from the architect who sought archaeological correctness when adopting them in modern designs. This specificity was significant because Strickland believed that the appeal of Greek architecture could be explained only in part by historical associations and emotional responses; ultimately, the most important "criterion" for judgment was "the nature of the architecture alone . . . which calls forth our admiration."[2]

EARLY PRACTICE

Walter commenced his independent practice around 1830, a time when publications on historic architecture from around the world were becoming increasingly available in America. Although he maintained an interest in many historic cultures, Walter held to Strickland's teaching that of all precedents available for study, "the soul-inspiring charms of Architecture" were to be found in "Greece alone"—although Walter, who never traveled to Greece, depended on books to discover them.[3]

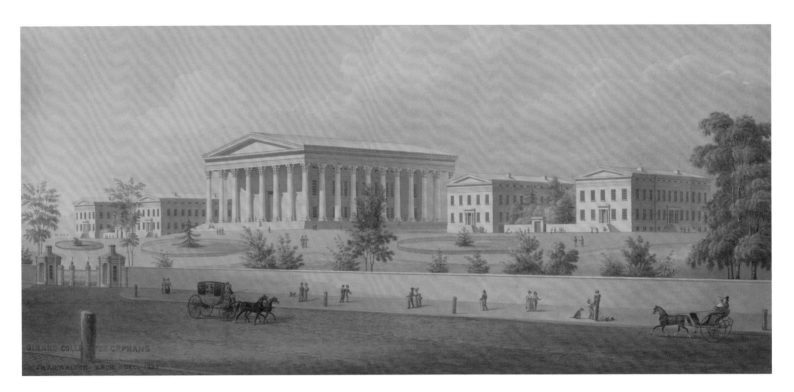

Figure 1 (top): Thomas U. Walter, Girard College, Philadelphia, Pennsylvania. Perspective rendering, 1835. (Thomas Ustick Walter Collection, Athenaeum of Philadelphia).

Figure 2 (bottom): Thomas U. Walter, United States Capitol, Washington, D.C. Design for Extension and New Dome, 1855. (Thomas Ustick Walter Collection, Athenaeum of Philadelphia).

Figure 3 (opposite): Ionic order of Palladio, from the notebook of Thomas U. Walter ca. 1830. (Thomas Ustick Walter Collection, Athenaeum of Philadelphia).

In his determination to achieve the architectural exactitude encouraged by Strickland, Walter compiled a collection of excerpts, notes, drawings, and data tables into a small notebook that was intended to be a personal guide to the precepts of classical architecture in general and the Greek orders in particular.[4] He depended on revered authors of the past and present to describe the canon of esteemed examples for reproduction, beginning with a three-page excerpt from John Haviland's *Builder's Assistant* (1818) on the method of drawing the elevation of the Greek Doric order. Additional architectural treatises, ranging from the classic *I quattro libri dell'architettura* by Andrea Palladio (1570) to the modern *A Dictionary of Arts and Sciences* by George Gregory (1806), completed this study.[5] Walter examined the Ionic order in similar depth, including directions for its accurate delineation according to specific examples presented by William Wilkins (*The Civil Architecture of Vitruvius*, 1809), Peter Nicholson (the Erectheum as recorded in the *Architectural Dictionary*, 1819), and Palladio [FIGURE 3]. After these lengthy studies of the Doric and Ionic, Walter's gloss on the third Greek order is noticeably slight, comprising only a short paragraph on the Corinthian order of the Monument of Lysicrates. Walter's focus on the Greek Doric and Ionic was consistent with the commonly-held idea that they were the most appropriate for American public buildings, which tended toward expressions of dignity and tranquility natural to the Doric and Ionic, respectively.[6]

By comparison, Walter's treatment of the Roman orders is marginal. He included two ink-wash renderings of the Tuscan order and a temple elevation. Walter recognized only the three developed in Greece as true orders; those associated with Rome were merely variations of the Greek originals.[7] Walter embraced the idea that Asher Benjamin expressed in the *Rudiments of Architecture:* the Doric, Ionic, and Corinthian were a kind of architectural "alphabet" while the Tuscan and Composite "amount to nothing more than different arrangements and combinations of their parts."[8] Given the universality of the orders, it was both impossible and undesirable for contemporaries to invent new ones. Walter also subscribed to this view, calling the Greek orders the "Alphabet of Classical Architecture." Contemporary architects had "no more need of a new one, than we have of additional letters in the formation of words or a new note in the musical scale."[9]

This dependence on precedent was a significant aspect of contemporary architectural design, even perceived as an essential aspect of the architectural culture of Walter's day: in 1835 George Wightwick wrote in the *Architectural Magazine*, "the present age is an age of selection and adaptation."[10] Borrowing from specific architectural precedents did not limit the architect's creative potential, but rather was an expected aspect of *originality,* which was more highly valued than *novelty,* given the nineteenth-century meaning of these terms. Whereas *novelty* expressed "newness, [a] state of being unknown in former times," *originality* was akin to a "fountain [or] source; that which gives beginning or existence."[11] An *original* architect borrowed discrete elements of approved examples to codify the overall soundness and harmony of a design, as an author might support the thesis of his essay with quotations from ancient texts. The use of such references made both writers and architects legible and persuasive. On the other hand, *novelty* was divorced from any preexisting system. As underscored by a contemporary writer in *Fraser's Magazine,* "to attain novelty, an architect has only to adopt the first whim that presents itself, but to be original demands either profound study or the most felicitous conception."[12] Novelty could offer only a temporal, possibly self-indulgent thrill and thus had little merit in the serious and permanent realm of civic architecture.

Walter absorbed these beliefs, understanding that even when significant portions of a building's elevations were culled from the pages of history, its overall design was as free from absolutes as the orders appeared to be bound by them. Walter needed to look no further than Strickland's Second Bank (1818), which recreates the Parthenon as accurately as was then possible in Philadelphia, to see the extent to which his teacher had to manipulate, change, redirect, alter, and invent to accommodate modern functions of the bank within the venerable precedent [FIGURE 4]. Strickland's facility in designing original buildings with exacting details studied from books would provide Walter the model of practice that shaped his early career.

GIRARD COLLEGE
Walter revealed the degree to which he intended to engage in the "profound study" required for architectural originality (as advocated by *Fraser's*) through his growing library, especially his purchase in March 1833 of the authoritative (and, at $75, costly) *Antiquities of Athens* by James Stuart and Nicholas Revett. These volumes became prized references, both necessitated by Walter's manner of design and financially enabled by his appointment as architect of Girard College—not coincidentally, also in March 1833. Walter pored through the *Antiquities* and other similar publications in the process of designing the country's most thoroughly Greek conception for the main hall of the College. This endeavor was enthusiastically supported by Nicholas Biddle, president of the Board of Trustees, who had famously proclaimed that "the two

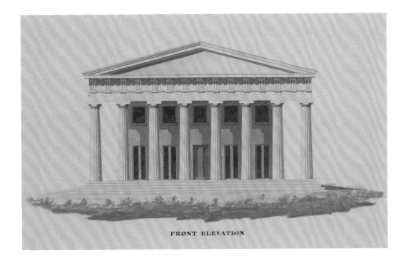

FRONT ELEVATION

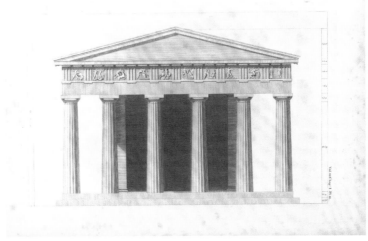

great truths in the world" were the Bible and Greek architecture.[13] As constructed, the three-story (97-feet-high) classroom building measured 160 x 217 feet in plan, and took the form of a great white marble temple complete with a peripteral colonnade [FIGURE 1]. Highly visible, supremely public and very expensive, the building was liable to attract significant public scrutiny and thus was not a place for capricious contributions by a young architect. Walter's was a truly *original* composition: for the colonnade, he chose the Corinthian order—rarely used by the Greeks—specifying the model provided by the Choragic Monument of Lysicrates that he recorded in his early notebook and now studied in the *Antiquities*. To conform to the scale of the college building, Walter designed its orders approximately five times taller than their original size, with columns of 6' diameter reaching a height of 55'; the capitals alone measured over eight feet tall.[14] Another original aspect of the design was the inclusion of four flanking buildings that served ancillary functions for the classroom building. Directed by his client to make them "as plain as possible," Walter turned again to the

Figure 4 (opposite): William Strickland, Second Bank of the United States, Philadelphia, PA. Principal elevation, 1818-24. (Olson Collection, Athenaeum of Philadelphia).

Figure 5A (top left): Thomas U. Walter, Andalusia, near Philadelphia, PA. Country seat of Nicholas Biddle, Esq., 1833. (Thomas Ustick Walter Collection, Athenaeum of Philadelphia).

Figure 5B (top right): Thesion, from *The Antiquities of Athens,* by Stuart and Revett, 1833. (Courtesy Hesburgh Libraries of Notre Dame's Architecture Library).

Figure 6A (bottom left): Thomas U. Walter, Hibernian Hall, Charleston, SC. 1832-41. (Library of Congress, Prints & Photographs Division, HABS).

Figure 6B (bottom right): Temple on the Ilussus, from *The Antiquities of Athens,* by Stuart and Revett, 1833. (Courtesy Hesburgh Libraries of Notre Dame's Architecture Library).

Antiquities and selected the Corinthian order of the Tower of the Winds, a model that was harmonious yet showed the order "in its simplest form."[15] Walter's concise quotations were thoroughly Greek, while the overall essay served the functional necessities of the school and the budget-consciousness of its Board of Trustees.[16]

Like the majority of his work during the 1830s, Girard College depended for its formal character on images from books that manifest the perfect and unassailable beauty of ancient Greek architecture. Walter explained the reasons for his trust in, and dependence on, Greek examples in his notes on the design of another project that he completed for the Grecophile Biddle: additions to his country estate, Andalusia (near Philadelphia, 1833) [FIGURE 5A]. After determining that the basic profile of his new façade matched the general proportions of a classical Greek hexastyle portico, Walter turned to the *Antiquities of*

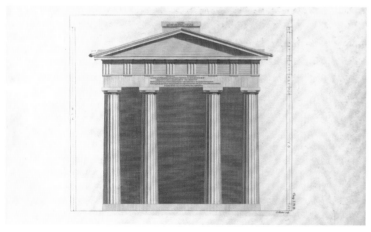

Figure 7A (top): Thomas U. Walter, Chester County Bank, Chester, PA. Perspective, 1836. (Thomas Ustick Walter Collection, Athenaeum of Philadelphia).

Figure 7B (bottom): Gate of Athena Archegetis, from The Antiquities of Athens, by Stuart and Revett, 1833. (Courtesy Hesburgh Libraries of Notre Dame's Architecture Library).

Figure 8 (opposite): Thomas U. Walter, Egyptian "orders" as illustrated in Lecture I, 1841. (Thomas Ustick Walter Collection, Athenaeum of Philadelphia).

Athens for a model, accepting the fact that the Greeks had "exhausted architectural beauty as it regards the use of columns." Thinking it was absurd to "endeavor to mend perfection," he adopted, without variation, the entire front of the Thesion, one of the "almost numberless examples already made perfect" [FIGURE 5B]. Walter believed that his process of selection, adoption, and application required a high degree of "real taste and talent:" he was no mere "copyist."[17] Walter followed a similar procedure in dozens of projects from the 1830s, including the Hibernian Hall (Charleston, SC 1832), inspired by the Temple on the Ilissus [FIGURES 6A AND 6B], and the Chester County Bank (West Chester, PA 1835), which recreates the entire tetrastyle Gate of Athena Archegetis [FIGURES 7A AND 7B]. Even with this consistent dependence on classical sources, Walter stressed that the architect should not thoughtlessly copy arbitrary examples, but should shrewdly judge all ancient evidence, sometimes even renouncing a precedent that might have been valuable to others. For instance, he noted that the angled volutes on corner capitals at St. Pancras Church, Tottenham, London (William Inwood, 1819-22) "look very bad although they are *à la Grec*, they are on this account above criticism, but I never can be persuaded to follow the Greeks in this barbarism."[18] Walter exercised personal judgment within a general deference for the Greek example, contributing to the originality of his architectural design. This broad scope continued to expand as his career progressed.

MID-CAREER TRANSITION

The narrow orthodoxy of Walter's early practice broadened by the 1840s as he placed increasing emphasis on exercising the principles, rather than recreating the particulars, of Greek architecture. At the same time, Walter began writing history and theory that positioned Greek accomplishments in a broader continuum of Western architectural history. Walter practiced the classical language with authority while admitting a greater number of historical styles (Egyptian, Italianate, Gothic) into his architectural practice. His maturing outlook denied the absolute hegemony of an ancient Greek canon, or "so many exact patterns . . . which the Architect must either copy line for line, or submit to the charge of ignorance or heresy."[19] Walter's changing attitude may have been inspired, in part, by the glut of buildings by lesser architects that betrayed rote mimicry of ancient examples—accurate but lifeless recreations of details regardless of their destination or context. He condemned such uninspired imitation as "labored imitations of . . . relics of Grecian genius" that were "as adverse to the spirit of classic art as it is tiresome and monotonous in its effects."[20]

Walter encouraged contemporary architects to "adapt examples from the antique to particular situations" to correct the problem of employing the orders without consideration of the character of the whole building.[21] He also considered the orders themselves more broadly. Rather than focus on their standard Hellenic nomenclature, he referred to them in more general terms as "general expressions" based on their relative proportions. These "natural grades of proportion" manifest a range of expression, from strength to lightness, separated by a "middle ground." Thus the "robust" (formerly Doric) and "elegant" (Corinthian) occupied the extremes flanking the "chaste"

(Ionic). These characterizations were so accommodating that they suggested to Walter the existence of similar standards in Egyptian architecture [FIGURE 8]; he believed these early "classes" of columns later inspired the true orders of the Greeks (and also later developments by the Romans).[22]

Within this range of relative proportion, which still admitted only three *genuine* orders, Walter located vast possibilities for diversity in the embellishment of each one. The ripest order for enhancement was the most naturally decorative, the "elegant" or Corinthian (also called the "foliate" version in the Egyptian tradition). The two ancient Greek examples that he used for the Girard College campus revealed the degree of variation possible within the single order: that of the Choragic Monument of Lysicrates is highly florid, especially in comparison to the simpler version from the Tower of the Winds. The inventive quality exhibited by the ancients encouraged moderns to devise new embellishments while remaining true to the proportional standards of the original order. Walter did just this in the design for the portico of the offices for the Philadelphia Contributionship Insurance Company (1835), as recorded by one of his assistants, who drew a parallel of three "elegant" orders, including one of Walter's invention, as part of his training in Walter's office [FIGURE 9].[23] Walter's design was not a new order, but rather a subtle variation on a standard set by the Greeks. This departure was an early example of the increasingly forceful originality that Walter would bring to the design of the orders by mid-century, the apex of his career.

THE CAPITOL

Walter's initial assignment as Architect of the Capitol was to design additions to the original building begun by William Thornton in 1793 and completed by Benjamin Latrobe (1803-17) and Charles Bulfinch (1818-29) [FIGURE 10]. Walter had no great admiration for the original design, which he described as a "mixture of Greek and Roman features in the details of its architecture which will ever deprive it of the reputation of being a monument of *pure* taste."[24] Yet the exterior of this hallowed hall was not the place for a bold display of novelty, even to correct earlier offenses against good taste. Compelled to harmonize his additions with the original structure, Walter designed wings that echoed the original building's scale, vertical rhythm and cornice line. Each wing is fronted by a broad flight of stairs flanked by cheek blocks, rising to a projecting Corinthian octastyle portico [FIGURES 11 AND 2]. In one important change, Walter sought a richer sculptural quality than the original pilaster order, which he replaced with freestanding columns in the porticos and links between the wings and original building. In his deeply considered study of the Capitol, Henry Hope Reed described Walter's changes to the precedent as achieving greater depth, sharpness, and stronger relief in both the sculptural quality of the capitals and the richness of the shafts, which are fluted. Instead of following the example of the extant columns, Walter looked to ancient principles that encouraged flutes in exterior applications.[25] With this small but significant change, Walter emphasized the richness of the Corinthian order with his own articulation while being deferential to the Capitol's original architecture [FIGURES 12A AND 12B].

Walter enjoyed greater freedom for originality in his designs for the building's interiors. The isolated legislative chambers and ceremonial passageways allowed him to be more inventive than he had been in the more deferential exercise of the façade designs. Significantly, in the detailing of the interiors, Walter relied not on print sources but, rather, on his natural intuition, long experience, and—as recorded by him for the first time—study from nature. Walter, the professed bibliophile, proudly claimed that he devised many of the designs for interior ornaments "without recourse to books at all."[26] Although Walter may have been influenced by the pervasive teachings of John Ruskin (and he did, at some point, collect Ruskin's works[27]), the two did not agree on many matters—such as Ruskin's demand for "truth" to materials, a principle seemingly disregarded in Walter's recreation of the Corinthian order (an element originally developed in masonry) in cast iron for the ornament of the Capitol dome.[28] Walter's new approach developed along with his relationship with art collector William Wilson Corcoran, who exposed him to the work of the Hudson River School and other "native" painters who celebrated the American landscape and its indigenous flora. Walter also had before him the example of Latrobe's well-known cornstalk columns in the vestibule of the Senate Chamber (1809) [FIGURE 13]. Two decades earlier Walter would probably have agreed with his teacher, Strickland, who in 1824 described this invention as a lamentable lapse of judgment;[29] but as a mature and accomplished architect, Walter was inspired by Latrobe's capitals to carry on the true Greek tradition that he believed encouraged development of particular expressive content within the overall character and form of the orders. Walter's version of the Corinthian capital in the Senate reception room conjoins magnolia blossoms, tobacco, and corn leaves rather than the ancient fleuron and acanthus.[30]

Exemplary among Walter's interiors in the Capitol is the Hall of Columns, the ceremonial entryway to the House of Representatives in the south wing [FIGURE 14]. Lining a broad corridor, twenty-eight

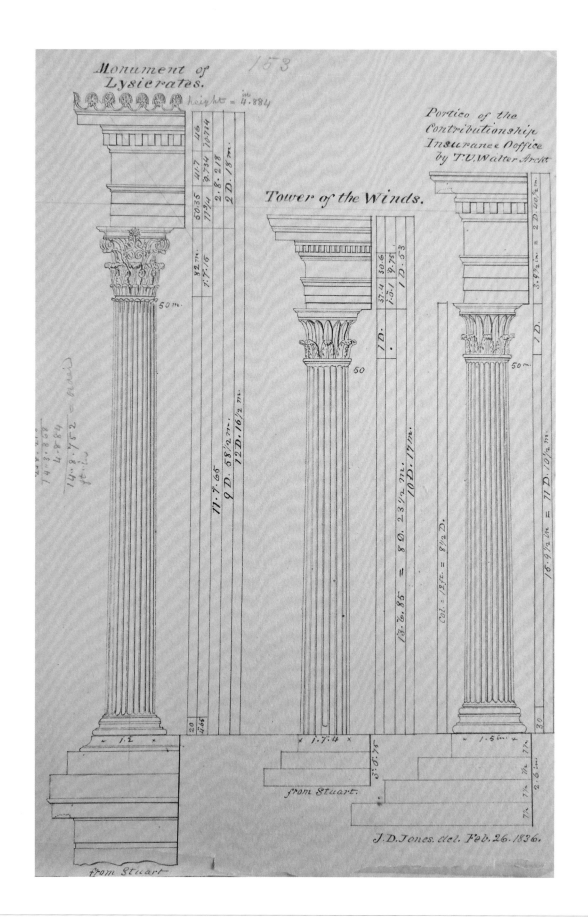

Monument of Lysicrates.

Tower of the Winds.

Portico of the Contributionship Insurance Office by T. U. Walter Archt

from Stuart.

from Stuart.

J. D. Jones. del. Feb. 26. 1836.

stop-fluted columns of white Massachusetts marble feature Walter's "American" version of the Corinthian order. Dividing the conventional bell shape in halves, Walter designed a row of acanthus leaves below a row of alternating thistles and tobacco leaves. Unlike the care he had taken twenty years earlier to reproduce the lines of the *Antiquities,* Walter now devised and drew the ornaments "from nature, by my own hand, in my own studio" [FIGURE 15]. Similarly, for the vestibule of the Senate Chamber, Walter integrated local flora that he had studied firsthand, calling the composition a "wholly original" version of the Corinthian order; its capital preserved the traditional bell shape, volutes, and acanthus leaves but introduced floral elements (tobacco and magnolia), which he had drawn "from nature" and from casts of blossoms [FIGURE 16].

In primary rooms like the Senate chamber, Walter's ornament was "original, or modifications of antique mouldings" that depended, for full effect, on comparison with the more canonical ornament that appeared in such less-important areas as the stairways and the Senate retiring room. Walter described this juxtaposition as "ancient colloca-tion," using a term from linguistics to underscore the role of the canonical models as foils to his modern works. Innovation for its own sake was mere swagger; by placing his designs in relation to clear ancient prece-dent, Walter could both honor his exemplars and prove the excellence of the modern age, while avoiding the novelty that would have brought attention only to him. Walter was proud of his accomplishment "for the sake of modern art, and for the credit of the nation." Although he had given up recreating Greek details out of books, he had not abandoned the Greeks themselves. Rather, Walter had mastered their methods so that he no longer stood behind Iktinos (or even Strickland), but now walked in "the course of the Ancients," writing, "I am much more desirous to think as they thought, than to do exactly as they did."[31]

LATER LIFE

Even after his retirement from Washington in 1865, Walter maintained his high standing in professional circles that provided opportunities for him to share his views in both private correspondence and public venues. In a letter to William Ware, who asked Walter's opinion about his plans for the new architecture program at MIT, Walter criticized academies that directed students to spend their time "chiefly occupied in drawing from classic examples of 'the orders' etc." rather than learning the principles of architecture that would encourage proper development within the longstanding traditions.[32] As president of the American Institute of Architects during the decade prior to his death in 1887, Walter had many opportunities to speak before his professional peers. In one such address he clearly expressed how much his thinking had changed from his days with Strickland. Walter observed, "The archi-tect of today is vastly different from the architect of a half a century ago" who "never forgot to introduce, wherever possible, the inevitable Greek portico drawn with the most scrupulous accuracy from Stuart's Athens, Chandler's Ionia, the *Antiquities of Attica,* or some other equally reliable authority." Since that time architects had learned to use ancient

Figure 9 (opposite): John D. Jones, Drawing of the "elegant" (Corinthian) orders. (Thomas Ustick Walter Collection, Athenaeum of Philadelphia).

Figure 10 (top): William Thornton, Benjamin Latrobe, and Charles Bulfinch, United States Capitol, Washington, D.C. View of East Front in 1846, prior to Thomas U. Walter's interventions. Daguerreotype by John Plumbe, 1846. (Library of Congress, Prints & Photographs Division).

Figure 11 (bottom): Thomas U. Walter, United States Capitol, Washington, D.C. Senate portico from southeast. (Photo by Anne Day).

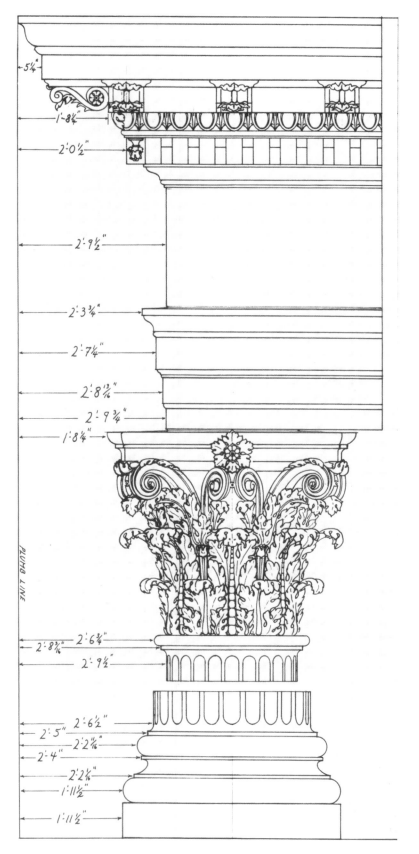

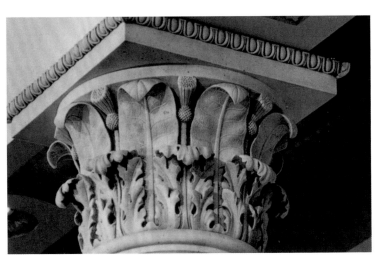

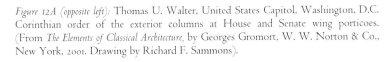

Figure 12A (opposite left): Thomas U. Walter, United States Capitol, Washington, D.C. Corinthian order of the exterior columns at House and Senate wing porticoes. (From *The Elements of Classical Architecture,* by Georges Gromort, W. W. Norton & Co., New York, 2001. Drawing by Richard F. Sammons).

Figure 12B (opposite top right): Thomas U. Walter, United States Capitol, Washington, D.C. Corinthian order of the exterior columns at House and Senate wing porticoes. (Photo by Anne Day).

Figure 13 (opposite bottom right): Benjamin Latrobe, United States Capitol, Washington, D.C. Corn-cob capitals in the Old East Senate Stairway, 1809. (Photo by Anne Day).

Figure 14 (top): Thomas U. Walter, United States Capitol, Washington, D.C. Hall of Columns in the House Wing. General view. (Photo by Anne Day).

Figure 15 (bottom left): Thomas U. Walter, United States Capitol, Washington, D.C. Hall of Columns in the House Wing. Detail of capital. (Photo by Anne Day).

Figure 16 (bottom right): Thomas U. Walter, United States Capitol, Washington, D.C. Vestibule of Senate Reception Room. Detail of capital. (Photo by Anne Day).

precedents "as suggestive" standards and "not as specimens to be servilely copied."[33] Although he had abandoned his earlier reliance on specific formal precedents, Walter thought that the use of classical principles was more relevant than ever. In his inaugural address as President of the AIA, Walter warned against the hasty rejection of all things traditional that he observed among contemporary architects, some of whom practiced extreme eclecticism after being provoked by lifeless simulations of Greek models. "Extravagant freaks of fancy" could be avoided by following "principles of law and order, evolved from the fragmentary remains of nationalities which have long since passed out of existence." Deep study of the ancient example, both its orders and its principles, assured that the present-day architect would abide by "the eternal fitness of things" and "the irrevocable principles of beauty," while still expressing a modern, creative spirit.[34]

Walter's first buildings reveal the efforts of a young architect who scrupulously adopted approved models to achieve the undeniable beauties that had not been eclipsed since the time of the ancients. In 1835 he wrote that a borrowed element—a capital or portico, for example—was like an "elegant quotation…beautifully interspersed with original ideas [as] in a well arranged oration."[35] The borrower still expressed original notions, but they were supported by the sanction of ancient authority. These were the quotations of a youth in training, learning to express his thoughts in an adopted language. In his maturity, Walter understood the orders as the architectural expressions of "principles that nature dictates," just as words were the verbal expression of similar natural conventions used by people to express individual thought.[36] Commanding these principles, the fully mature architect could comfortably devise new expressions—modern idioms based in timeless meaning—as the ancients had done, believing that an architect who had carefully studied the ancients for decades might achieve an equivalent greatness in his own compositions. True respect for the ancients meant adopting not only their formal paradigms but also the approach to original design that they modeled in their diverse works. In this pursuit Walter could exercise "ancient taste perfected by modern hands."[37] The youthful architect might excerpt quotations from established masters, but the mature architect commanded a language and used it to communicate his own convictions. ❦

Jhennifer A. Amundson, Ph.D., is a professor at Judson University in Elgin, Illinois, where she teaches the history and theory of architecture. She is the editor of Thomas Ustick Walter: The Lectures on Architecture *(Athenaeum of Philadelphia, 2006) and the author of a forthcoming monograph on Walter.*

NOTES

1. In his lectures, Strickland referred to such authors as William Chambers and Palladio. Although not pure Grecophiles, their books (available to Strickland for purchase in America or in Philadelphia libraries) included the canonical versions of the orders that Strickland discussed in these lectures.

2. Strickland's lectures are recorded in a transcript by Reuben Haines III, "Notes on William Strickland's Architectural Lectures at the Franklin Institute, 1824-25," Box 90, folder 65, Wyck Papers, American Philosophical Society, Philadelphia. See also Agnes Gilchrist, *William Strickland, Architect and Engineer* (Philadelphia: University of Pennsylvania Press, 1950), 41.

3. Thomas U. Walter, January 16, 1835, Journal 1834-36, Thomas Ustick Walter Collection, Athenaeum of Philadelphia (hereafter "Walter Collection, Athenaeum"). Walter did travel through Europe in 1838, where he studied modern Greek architecture in Great Britain and France, but he always preferred to use the original Greek models, in printed form, to inspire his architectural designs.

4. Walter, Notebook, Box 1, 122-M-005, Walter Collection, Athenaeum.

5. Throughout this paper, the precise edition has been noted when cited in Walter's papers, which is often the case. It is not so for Walter's Palladio, many versions of which might have been available to him through personal loans as well as in Philadelphia's many libraries.

6. Among other sources, Walter read this idea in Asher Benjamin (*The Rudiments of Architecture*, Boston: Munroe and Francis, 1814), 35. In his first decade of practice, the great majority of Walter's buildings that include classical ornament feature either Doric or Ionic (although one of the few applications of Corinthian, Girard College, is a significant anomaly).

7. Although in his early career Walter may have disregarded the Composite order due to the practical concern for locating American sculptors with the skills to carve its complicated forms and his general distaste for Roman architecture, later in life Walter denied its status as an order. As a "union of the Ionic and the Corinthian" it expressed no individual principles that would distinguish it as a true order. In a lecture of 1841 he explained that the misnomer was of recent origin: "The dignified appellation of orders has been given to them by writers of comparatively modern date, without either reason, or authority to warrant it." See *Thomas U. Walter: The Lectures on Architecture, 1841-53*, ed. Jhennifer A. Amundson (Philadelphia: Athenaeum of Philadelphia: 2006), 109 (Lecture III: 13-14).

8. Benjamin, *Rudiments*, 20, 32.

9. Walter, Journal 1834-36, Box 19 122-M-263, Walter Collection, Athenaeum.

10. Published in England, the *Architectural Magazine* was popular among American architects, including Walter, who held a subscription. See George Wightwick in the *Architectural Magazine*, (London: 1835), 344, also quoted in Roger A. Kindler, "Periodical Criticism 1815-40: Originality in Architecture," *Architectural History* 17 (1974), 25.

11. *Johnson's English Dictionary* (Boston: Perkins & Marvin, 1830).

12. "Architectural Design and Decoration," *Fraser's Magazine* (February, 1830): 72. Quoted in Kindler, 24.

13. Nicholas Biddle quoted in Edward Biddle, "Girard College," *Proceedings of the Numismatic and Antiquarian Society of Pennsylvania* 27 (1916): 201. The celebrated Greek design for Girard College reflects a significant revision of Walter's original, competition-winning design and was greatly encouraged by Biddle's preferences. See Bruce Laverty, Michael J. Lewis, and Michelle Taillon Taylor, *Monument to Philanthropy: The Design and Building of Girard College, 1832-1848* (Philadelphia: Girard College, 1998).

14. Although Walter did not design the columns to have entasis, as those of a classical Greek temple would have, he did increase the diameter of the corner columns (by 1-½ inches), "for the purpose of overcoming the apparent reduction in their size arising from their insulated position." Walter, "Final Report of the Architect," in *A Description of Girard College for Orphans* (Philadelphia: 1848), 9.

15. Walter, March 2, 1835, "Girard College Correspondence," 122-M-043, Walter Collection, Athenaeum.

16. Walter was bound from the start to serve the difficult plan stipulated in Stephen Girard's will and, with time, the budget-consciousness of the Board of Trustees, which grew in response to rising public concerns over the long construction process and unprecedented costs required by the massive building.

17. Walter, January 13, 1835, Journal 1834-36, Box 19 122-M-263, Walter Collection, Athenaeum.

18. Walter, European Journal, Box 25, 122-M-487, Walter Collection, Athenaeum. Although instances of the diagonal volute could be found in Greece, and thus the detail was technically *"à la Grec,"* it was most notably used by the Romans during the Empire and later popularized by Scamozzi, tarnishing it with Roman and Renaissance associations that further soured Walter's assessment.

19. Walter held that "Modern rules "were made to fit the ancient orders, and not the orders to confirm to the rules." *Walter: The Lectures,* ed. Amundson, 80 (Lecture II: 26).

20. He continued, "yet these 'classic models,' no matter how absurd their application, may be tolerated and even justified, on the ground of 'authority.'" Walter, "The Orders," *Journal of the Franklin Institute* 1, no. 3 (April 1841): 194-96.

21. *Walter: The Lectures,* ed. Amundson, 109 (Lecture III: 14-15).

22. In his first lecture Walter explained that the "three general classes" of Egyptian columns bore "distinctive characters…as decidedly marked as those of the Greek or Roman orders;" he allowed that, when paired with their architraves, they "might with propriety be called Egyptian orders." His Egyptian *parallel* included specific examples from the Île d'Elephantine ("robust," with a proportional relationship of 4:1), Dendera ("medium" or "Isis order," 1:6) and Karnak ("foliated order," 1:7). In his second lecture he reiterated the idea that the Greek orders maintain the "same constituent principles as the columnar Architecture of the Egyptians," which must be their source. *Walter: The Lectures,* ed. Amundson, 42-44 (Lecture I: 17-20) and 76 (Lecture II: 17).

23. John D. Jones, "A Sketch on Architecture by a Student, Philadelphia 1836," Walter Collection, Athenaeum.

24. *Walter: The Lectures,* ed. Amundson, 188 (Lecture V: 32-33).

25. Henry Hope Reed, *The United States Capitol: Its Architecture and Decoration* (New York: W. W. Norton & Company, 2005), 61.

26. Letter, Walter to Joseph B. Varnum Jr., January 23, 1863. Letterbooks, Walter Collection, Athenaeum.

27. For more information about Walter's library, see Jhennifer A. Amundson, " 'Vast Avenues to Knowledge': Thomas Ustick Walter's Books," in *American Architects and Their Books, 1840-1915,* ed. Kenneth Hafertepe and James F. O'Gorman (Amherst: University of Massachusetts Press, 2007): 63-94. At the time of his retirement in 1865, Walter's library included Ruskin's *Lectures on Architecture and Painting* (1854) and *The Seven Lamps of Architecture* (1849).

28. Indeed, for decades Walter had designed orders and other architectural features in a variety of materials, including stone, cast iron and wood, always directing the latter two materials to be painted to appear as stone (most recently with the cast iron capitals of the Chester County Courthouse, designed in 1846).

29. Strickland remarked, "The Architect flattered himself that he had made a hit and established a new order of Columns. In this instance the eye was satisfied with the novelty, but not so the mind." See Gilchrist, 38.

30. Reed, 121.

31. Walter, Diary, January 26, 1855, and Letter to Joseph B. Varnum Jr., January 23, 1863, both Walter Collection, Athenaeum. When Walter refers to the "Ancients" he indicates the Greeks, who continued to provide the model of chasteness and simplicity that Walter followed in principle, regardless of particular style. For this reason he could accommodate his own new designs, as well as historically Roman forms (even a dome) within his "Grecian" sensibilities. Because of his devotion to simplicity and restraint, likewise, Walter could not abide the florid and exuberant Renaissance-inspired fresco decoration added to the Capitol under direction of the engineer Montgomery C. Meigs.

32. Walter never suggested that students should abandon the study of the orders specifically (or historical traditions more generally) because mastering general principles allowed architects to properly invent *original* designs. He criticized the adoption of motifs as ornamental devices divorced from the context of their overall traditions. He railed against this practice, and the related fashion of blending cosmetic features from different cultures in single buildings, which became increasingly popular during the 1870s. Walter, letter to William R. Ware, September 29, 1874, Letterbooks, Walter Collection, Athenaeum.

33. Walter, undated address, Box 20, 122-M-287, Walter Collection, Athenaeum.

34. Walter, address for AIA annual meeting, Boston, 1877, Walter Collection, Athenaeum.

35. Walter, Diary, January 13, 1835, Walter Collection, Athenaeum.

36. *Walter: The Lectures,* ed. Amundson, 79 (Lecture II: 24-25).

37. Walter, Diary, January 27, 1855, Walter Collection, Athenaeum.

The author wishes to thank Bruce Laverty, Gladys Brooks Curator of Architecture at the Athenaeum of Philadelphia, for facilitating access to the documents and drawings in the Walter Collection published here.

A Greek Revival in the Eternal City
PROJECTS FOR THE NATIONAL STADIUM IN ROME 1906-11

By Raffaele Giannantonio

Designs for the 1911 National Stadium in Rome reveal the mutable relationships linking architecture, history, identity, and politics—and how adaptation of the classical language reflects perceived continuities and ruptures between past and present.

Classical architecture offers the designer diverse characters that may be used to express different intentions. Such characters may be evoked by general building configurations or types as well as by elevation features or decorative detail. The use of varied strains of the classical language was especially nuanced in the late nineteenth and early twentieth centuries, when architects sought to embody newly emerging national identities by adapting to present needs models drawn from the past. The story of the National Stadium in Rome, as presented here, reveals how architectural conceptions grounded in history intersected with present-day cultural and political aspirations and how the universal values of classicism became intertwined with local or national traditions. In Rome, this process naturally involved the further consideration of the architect's relationship to a distant past whose vestiges remained potent symbols of Italian identity.[1]

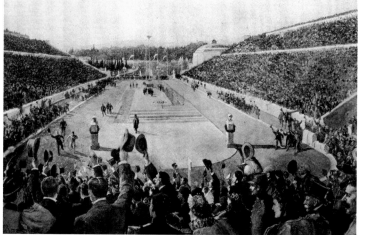

Figure 1 (above): The Panathenaic Stadium, Athens. The victory of Spyridon Louis in the marathon shown in a period illustration (April 10, 1896).

The urge to define that national identity began with the constitution of the unified Italian state in 1861 and became a matter of public interest in many different cultural manifestations, including in architecture related to sport. From an elite activity of the leisure class, sport gradually became a mass phenomenon by the end of the nineteenth century, thanks in part to the "invention" of the modern Olympic Games by Baron Pierre de Coubertin in 1896, celebrated by the reconstruction of the Panathenaic Stadium in Athens, venue of the ancient games. [Figure 1] In 1911 new stadiums were opened in Turin and Rome as part of the International Exposition held to celebrate the fiftieth anniversary of Unification with sites split between the first and last capitals of Italy. The stadiums, both full of symbolic resonance, were born from two completely different architectural conceptions.

The cyclopean Stadium of Turin represented the typological antithesis of the one constructed in Rome in the same year, with which it shared the brevity of its existence [Figure 2].[2] As conceived by Vittorio Eugenio Ballatore di Rosana and Ludovico Gonella, the Turin stadium was to be "the gathering place of the people and the center around which the different sporting events would take place." Thanks to its dimensions, the Turin stadium was celebrated by the press as "the vastest in the world."[3] In response to this theme, the designers turned to the scheme of the ancient Roman amphitheater, shaping an elliptical plan whose axes measured 204 by 360 meters. (In comparison, the ancient Flavian Amphitheater in Rome, better known as the Coliseum, occupied an ellipse whose axes measured 191 by 223 meters.)

The triumphal entrance and the royal box faced one another down the central axis. According to Daniele Donghi, the "ten kilometers" of tiered seating hosted 24,000 seated spectators, or over 40,000 standing.[4] At the top was to be a portico that ran between little towers intended to divide the cavea into distinct sectors. A very innovative aspect of the stadium was the structural design, entirely in reinforced concrete, realized by the engineer Giovanni Antonio Porcheddu, an Italian pioneer in this technology. The sculptor Giovanni Battista Alloati modeled groups of equestrian statues, also realized in concrete. In the end, the Turin stadium design suffered numerous cost-saving simplifications during construction and its intended sumptuous decoration cast in the classical style was replaced by a language limited to the expression of the reinforced concrete skeleton in a tone of cold and off-putting modernity. [FIGURE 3] The exposed structural members on the side walls and the severe citation of the ancient imperial box (pulvinar) might have seemed an anticipation of the later Rationalist style, had the presence of the two sculptural groups by Alloati not brought to mind the "Greco-Roman style renewed by the architect Bellatore di Rosana and the engineer Gonella"[5] that the imposed economies negated.

Differently, the origins of the project for a National Stadium in Rome lie early in the twentieth century with Bruto Amante's proposal to build a new stadium on the ruins of the ancient Circus Maximus. Amante was the son of the scholar and Senator Errico Amante, one of the most important figures in the movement for national unification in Southern Italy. The younger Amante inherited his father's interest in ancient Rome, as revealed by his given name (i.e., "Brutus"). He was the author of numerous historical studies, including his book *The Birth of Rome* (1879), and held high positions in the Ministry of Public Instruction. As Secretary to the Minister Francesco De Sanctis, a close friend of his father, Amante was well-connected politically and this proved helpful in advancing his initiative for the new stadium.

As President of the National Scholastic Federation of Physical Education (FSNEF), Amante conceived his initiative in May 1906 while attending the convention organized in Athens on the occasion of the intermediate Olympic Games (held between the two official editions at St. Louis and London).[6] Amante represented the Ministry of Public Instruction and was a member of the Committee for the Panhellenic Games chaired by Luigi Lucchini, President of the National Institute for the Advancement of Physical Education in Italy (INEF). The venue of the Athens Games was again the Panathenaic Stadium, called *Kallimarmaro* for the precious marble used in its construction, but which had been abandoned for centuries. It was definitively restored in 1895 in order to host the first modern Olympic Games, held the following year.[7] The restoration was carried out by the architect Anastasios Metaxas, a member of the Olympic organizing committee and concurrently a competitor in target shooting[8] [FIGURE 4].

In Britain, sport had been a popular pursuit for a long time, but in Italy at the start of the twentieth century it was just taking its first steps. In fact, the newly-unified state recognized the great political and propaganda value of sport rather later than other European countries. For example, gymnastic exercise was required in schools in Denmark by 1804, but was introduced in Italy only in 1878. At that time, sport was pursued primarily by the aristocracy and upper middle class, unlike in England, where the leisure and recreational activity of the urban working class benefitted from a long-established tradition. In Italy, in the years before the First World War, the attitude was generally one of diffidence:

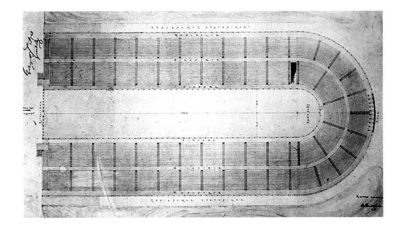

Figure 2 (top): Vittorio Eugenio Ballatore di Rosana and Ludovico Gonella, The Stadium, Turin, 1911. Aerial perspective of the project. (From Treves, Guido (ed.), *Le esposizioni del 1911: Roma, Torino, Firenze: rassegna illustrata delle mostre indette nelle tre capitali per solennizzare il cinquantenario del Regno d'Italia,* Milan: Fratelli Treves, 1911, p. 47.)

Figure 3 (middle): Vittorio Eugenio Ballatore di Rosana and Ludovico Gonella, Stadium, Turin, 1911. Photograph of the exterior upon completion of the structure. (Tummers Tijs, D'Eletto Clino, *Storia degli Stadi d'Italia illustrata da cartoline d'epoca,* [?], Tesink, 2007, p. 45.)

Figure 4 (bottom): Plan reconstruction of the Panathenaic Stadium, Athens, as it appeared in antiquity. (www.panathenaicstadium.gr).

the philosopher Benedetto Croce labelled as a "false ideal" the myth of sport exalted by Friedrich Nietzsche in Germany and Maurice Barrès in France. The political Left was generally uninterested: one of the fathers of the Socialist Party, Filippo Turati, thought organized sport "stupid and aristocratic." After an initial indifference, the Catholic Church at the turn of the century recognized the educational potential of sport and sought to transform what were seen as elite activities into a popular pursuit by creating local associations united in the Federation of Italian Catholic Sports Associations (FASCI). It was this Catholic sports movement that later resisted the forceful advance of Fascism, which for its part confronted the Catholic associations in a battle for the loyalties of Italian youth. Whereas, at the end of the nineteenth century, only equitation, fencing, and target shooting could count on a strong public following in Italy, interest increased in the early 1900s as sports like football (soccer) and cycling spread quickly—so much so that in 1904 the International Olympic Committee designated Rome as the site of the fourth edition of the Games.[9] Despite the enthusiasm shown by De Coubertin and the support of the King, however, the cost of organizing the Games and the rivalry between the cities of Milan and Turin forced the Italian government to decline the invitation.

Disappointed, Amante sought to address the grave lack of sporting facilities in Italy[10] and, with the motto "Hellas and Rome!" launched the idea of matching in the city of the Caesars "the splendid example of the resurrection of the Panathenaic Stadium," by reconstructing "that Circus Maximus, which was the epilogue of the city's glorious history from the first king onward...."[11] Amante understood that the realization of such a symbolic structure necessitated a new culture of sport involving the schools, "the true *consortium vitae* of the young." For this purpose, in June 1906 he led the formation of the FSNEF which, taking inspiration from the poet Juvenal, adopted the name *Virides*.[12]

Amante explained his idea at the Congress of Women's Physical Education in Milan the following September[13] and launched a general appeal in which he elaborated the "patriotic and educational goals" justifying the creation of a new National Stadium. The celebrations of the Fiftieth Anniversary of the proclamation of the Kingdom of Italy in 1911 seemed an opportune moment to realize the project, and a law passed July 11, 1907 restricting the use of the land surrounding the Circus Maximus site[14] urged "bringing back to light and to the admiration of the world the remains of the most sumptuous of the circuses of Rome."[15] In his publication, *The National Stadium in the Circus Maximus*, Amante proposed a project inspired by that completed in Athens in 1896; that is, to construct a new structure in the ancient Circus combining the architectural features of the Greek stadium and the Roman circus.

THE STADIUM AND THE CIRCUS: TYPES AND HISTORIES

The boundaries between these two architectural types have long been indistinct: the Greek stadiums were primarily intended for gymnastic competitions and foot races as part of religious festivals, while the Roman circuses were the venues primarily of horse and chariot races and gladiatorial contests as public entertainments. The circus has often been viewed as the Roman version of the Greek hippodrome, although the resemblance is limited to the plan configuration.[16] In Rome, in fact, athletic competitions passed from the religious sphere to that of *ludus*, or sport, and therefore from the sponsorship of the aristocracy to that of the businessmen who, for the purpose of improving the quality of the spectacle and the condition of the spectators, constructed permanent seating and provided additional services and facilities. For this reason, throughout the Romanized Greek world between the second and third centuries, the hippodromes, originally simple running tracks of beaten earth, were transformed into monumental structures on the model of the Roman circus.[17]

The most important difference in plan between the circus and the stadium was in the short side opposite the semi-circular end: in the stadium, this end was open and served as the public entrance; in the circus, it was closed by a broad arc housing the starting cages for the horses (*carceres*). The circus was also characterized by the *spina*, the *euripo*, and the *metae* in the center of the arena (see Note 24), and the length of the track was almost double that of the stadium. In spite of these differences, as Amante records, the term "stadium" was used in both Greek and Latin between the second and third centuries in the eastern provinces of the Empire to refer to structures in which chariot races took place, as well as those in which the *munera* (gladitorial fights) and *venationes* (fights between men and animals) were held.[18]

Actually, the stadium—the Greek monument par excellence—was little known by the Romans until the Imperial age, probably because of the simplicity of the structural systems used. At the beginning of their history the most important examples, like the stadiums of Olympia, Delphi, and Nemea, did not have stone steps for spectator seating but usually wooden benches, as seen in an inscription about the stadium of Delphi. Elsewhere, as in Epidauros and Delos, the stepped seating was arranged only on one side of the slope into which the stadium was carved. Complete and permanent *caveæ* appeared only between the first and second centuries BC, as at Delphi, where between 166 and 177 Herod Atticus built seats in the local limestone. The Roman model of the stadium was not a decisive factor because, besides the examples just cited, seating in stone had already been constructed in the Hellenistic age at Rhodes, Cos, and Dodona.[19] Roman influence was more significant in the evolution of the type in Asia Minor, as demonstrated by the structure at Nysa that Strabo calls *stadio-anfiteatro* because of its semi-circular plan at both

short ends.[20] Additionally, at the stadium of Aphrodisias in Caria, the first phase of which can be dated to the end of the first and the beginning of the second century, both short ends were semi-circular and the long sides were slightly curved to give the audience a better view.

Suetonius considered the first stadium constructed in Rome to be the temporary structure erected in the Campo Marzio to honor the triumph of Ceasar Augustus in 46 AD,[21] while, according to Amante, the first permanent stadium was the one constructed by Domitian between 86 and 90 AD to host the athletic games of the *certamen Capitolinum*, which he himself instituted in honor of Jupiter.[22] The arena of this structure, which corresponds to the current Piazza Navona, was 275 meters long (or one and a half times the length of an Olympic stadium) and 54 meters wide internally. The track was completely free except for the accessories needed for the games; the principal entrance was at the center of the semi-circular end and marked by a wide arch preceded by a monumental portico, while two secondary entrances opened on the long sides. The external façade was on two levels with arches framed by half-columns in the familiar fornix motif: the lower level employing the Ionic and the upper probably the Corinthian order. This upper level corresponded to the continuous portico *(mtænianum)* at the top of the seating.

Despite becoming one of the principal meeting places of Rome, the structure later fell out of favor with the population, which believed the "Greek" games immoral, as well as with the emperor, who was known to be excessively interested in the gladiatorial fights. Throughout Italy the Greek-style gymnastic games found a limited audience and, as a consequence, between the second and third centuries, stadiums were superseded by amphitheaters and circuses. In the former Magna Grecia the only stadium of architectural importance was that at Pozzuoli constructed by Antoninus Pius for the games he himself instituted in honor of his predecessor, Hadrian. Although the grand dimensions of the arena conformed to the circus type, the curvature of both short ends meant that it was intended for both athletic competitions and the games associated with the circus.

Figure 5 (opposite): Circus Maximus, Rome, in its most monumental form in the third century AD. Plan. (From Gros, P., *L'architecture romaine, 1. Les monuments publics*, Paris: Picard, 1996, p. 312)

Figure 6 (above): The Circus Maximus in its ancient urban context. View of the model of Rome in the time of Constantine. (Museo della civiltà romana, Rome.)

Amante's proposal took inspiration from the large number of circuses in ancient Rome, which, in addition to the Circus Maximus, included the Flaminio (or Apollo) and those of Alexander Severus, Hadrian, Caius, Domitian, Flora, Maxentius, and Sallust.[23] After describing the characteristics of the type based on the nineteenth-century treatise of Luigi Canina,[24] Amante proposed the reconstruction of the Circus Maximus, the oldest and grandest of the circuses of Rome and sited in the Murcia valley between the Palatine and Aventine hills [FIGURES 5 AND 6]. According to tradition, the Etruscan kings Tarquinius Priscus and Tarquinius Superbus erected the first stadium structure on the site in the sixth century B.C.[25] but, even though surrounded by religious buildings, it did not have a monumental character[26] and its functional characteristics were defined only after the middle of the fourth century B.C.[27]

In 46 B.C., Julius Caesar enlarged the Circus, but only with the advent of the imperial age would it take on a truly monumental character. Agrippa dressed the *spina* in marble decorated with bronze dolphins, while Augustus installed the obelisk of Ramses, constructed the royal box (*pulvinar*) on the side facing the Palatine, and the monumental entrance to the circus (*porta triumphalis*) on the side opposite the starting gates for the races (*carceres*).[28] This is how the complex looked to Dionysus of Halicarnassus, who in his *Roman Antiquities* described with admiration the portico that ran around the entire cavea of three tiers and seating 150,000 spectators in all—an astonishing number compared to the other venues for spectacles in the *Urbs*.[29] Fires in the

Figure 7 (above): Giovanni Battista Piranesi, "Veduta degli Avanzi delle Case de Cesari sul Palatino,", from *Le antichità Romane* (1784).

Figure 8 (opposite top): G. Magni and G. Podesti, Project for the Stadium at the Circus Maximus, Rome, plan, 1908. (From *Progetto per lo Stadio Massimo Nazionale sull'area del Circo Massimo*, a cura di *Virides*, Federazione Scolastica Nazionale Educazione Fisica, Roma, Stabilimento Fratelli Capaccini, 1909, p. 23.)

Figure 9 (opposite middle): G. Magni and G. Podesti, Project for the Stadium at the Circus Maximus, Rome, principal elevation, 1908. (From *Progetto per lo Stadio Massimo Nazionale sull'area del Circo Massimo*, a cura di *Virides*, Federazione Scolastica Nazionale Educazione Fisica, Roma, Stabilimento Fratelli Capaccini, 1909, p. 25.)

Figure 10 (opposite bottom): Project for the Stadium at the Circus Maximus, Rome, aerial perspective, 1908. (From *Progetto per lo Stadio Massimo Nazionale sull'area del Circo Massimo*, a cura di *Virides*, Federazione Scolastica Nazionale Educazione Fisica, Roma, Stabilimento Fratelli Capaccini, 1909, p. 26.)

first century offered opportunities to make the structure even more monumental: Caligula and Claudius rebuilt the *carceres* in marble and the *metæ* in gilded bronze, Nero increased the capacity to 250,000 spectators, and Titus enriched the Circus with a new triumphal entrance of three arches of the fornix type and added sculptural decoration to the entire *spina*.[30] In the *Panegyric of Trajan*, Pliny the Younger describes the Circus at the beginning of the second century, praising the majesty of the gigantic masonry structure at the foot of the Palatine;[31] indeed, the arena floor—at 580 meters long and 79 meters wide—was twelve times larger than that of the Coliseum.

A PROPOSED NATIONAL STADIUM AT THE CIRCUS MAXIMUS

It's important to notice that Amante chose the Circus Maximus as the preferred site for the proposed National Stadium, despite the fact that the archeologist Rodolfo Lanciani, whom he had consulted, had advised him to consider the Circus of Maxentius instead, since it was "well preserved." Amante was not convinced by Lanciani's opinion, noting that the conservation of the Circus of Maxentius was likely due to its distance from the center of Rome.[32] Amante argued that his program foresaw a new stadium that would rise on the archeological ruins and adapt the original typology to modern needs; moreover, at the Circus Maximus, the few archeological remains would allow a greater freedom in the "reconstruction." Indeed, it would be enough to demolish the buildings of the Societa' del Gas on the Aventine and the modest tenement buildings on the side of the Palatine to reconstruct the image depicted by Piranesi in one of his most famous engravings [FIGURE 7].

Importantly, the Circus Maximus could accommodate the activities historically associated with both the circus and the stadium, making it more suitable for the diverse competitions of a modern Olympics. As we have seen, this was not without ancient precedent: Suetonius and Dio Cassio reported how in antiquity the Circus Maximus hosted not only chariot races but also the *quinquertium*, the Roman equivalent of the Greek *pentathlon*,[33] exercises that for Amante constituted "the holy and healthy objective of the new generations, the truly educational element," and thus appropriately aligned with the aims of the anniversary celebrations of the Italian state. However, Amante was under no illusion that the structure would be completed in time for the 1911 events and proposed that, in that case, the immense arena capable of holding 140,000 persons could be temporarily fenced in, setting a "strict architectural line" on the site that, he believed, would have been built upon in any case.

In January 1908, Amante presented his publication *Lo Stadio Nazionale nel Circo Massimo* to the King, and the proposal to construct the new building "possibly" on the ruins of the ancient structure[34] received the support of, among others, the poet Gabriele d'Annunzio, the archaeologist Giacomo Boni, the sculptor Ettore Ferrari, and the art historian Adolfo Venturi. Particular importance was attributed to the positive opinion expressed by the sculptor Vito Pardo in his capacity as Director General of the Italian branch of *Audax*, the famous association of cycling enthusiasts.[35] Amante assembled his team, which included Lanciani as a consultant, along with the architects Giulio

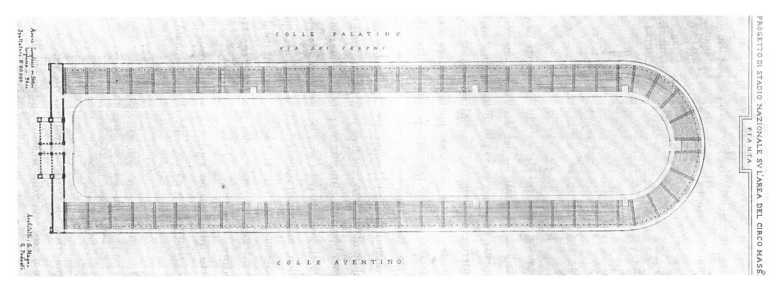

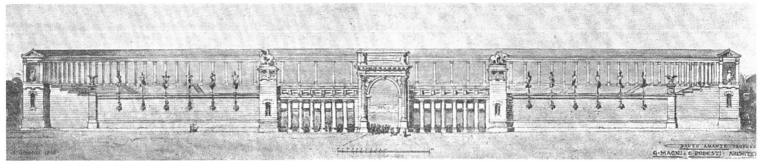

Magni and Giulio Podesti,[36] and on June 18, 1908, the "illustrious Roman architects" presented their project for the "reconstruction" of the Circus Maximus according to the archaeological indications supplied by Lanciani [FIGURE 8].[37]

The structure proposed by Amante had an ideal didactic value because it was intended, in the first instance, to host schoolchildren's competitions. However, while wanting to follow the example of the Panathenaic Stadium at Athens, he suggested for Rome a modern reconstruction not of the stadium type, but of the circus. The intention to reconcile the two types is apparent in all the studies for the project, and Podesti and Magni's proposal was an attempted synthesis of the architecture of the Greek stadium and that of the Roman circus in the form of a free reconstruction of the Circus Maximus. They retained the U-shaped plan and the same dimensions as the ancient structure but, disregarding the archaeological data, they omitted the monumental entrance at the semi-circular end and, at the opposite end, designed an entrance very different from the circus type. Here they proposed a great triumphal arch of *Beaux-Arts* taste, with undecorated walls to either side [FIGURE 9].

The arena floor was to occupy 50,000 square meters, the tiers of seats hold 60,000 spectators, and the portico at the top level accommodate another 10,000 standees. Below the *cavea* they planned vast halls for locker rooms, stables, and services, as well as caretakers' homes, management and administration offices, and restaurants [FIGURE 10]. In the end, the two architects estimated the costs for the realization of the work at not more than five million lire— a sum so high it immediately defeated the initiative.[38] In the end, something like Amante's proposal was realized as part of the 1911 Exposition, whose site in Rome strad-

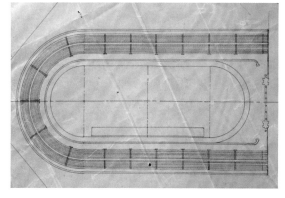

dled the Tiber on the north side of the city, but with this change in site the National Stadium lost any reference to the Circus Maximus and became, instead, a re-evocation of the Panathenaic Stadium in Athens.

THE NATIONAL STADIUM OF 1911

It was not clear in practical terms how Amante's proposal would have incorporated the archeological remains of the ancient Circus, and these perplexities prompted a parallel initiative on the part of the INEF, which the previous April had commissioned the architect Marcello Piacentini and the sculptor Vito Pardo (despite his earlier endorsement of Amante's proposal) to design "a concrete project responsive to technical, artistic, and financial considerations."[39] A survey was taken of persons "competent and eminent in the fields of archeology and art" to ask "if it were advisable to reconstruct one of the ancient circuses" or, rather,

"if it were more appropriate to construct a new, modern stadium on the site of the ancient Circus Maximus, suppressing every vestige of it." Because the great majority of respondents thought it more correct "to respect this vestige of Roman grandeur and to erect on an open site a stadium corresponding to modern needs," the INEF endorsed the project of Piacentini and Pardo and decided to realize it in the area along the Viale Flaminio where "all the sporting life of the Capital" would soon be centered. But in the meantime, the Mayor had conferred the same commission on the chief city engineer, Angelo Guazzaroni, and therefore, in 1910 the INEF and the City wisely commissioned Piacentini, Pardo, and Guazzaroni to undertake the project jointly in order to get construction underway quickly.[40] Every link with the Circus Maximus was finally dissolved in the design by Piacentini and Pardo, after which the city administration and INEF definitively abandoned Amante's proposal.[41]

Unlike Magni and Podesti, Piacentini designed the National Stadium at the beginning of his career, which had started in the office of his architect father Pio, who advised him to establish business relations with the other professionals who frequented his studio, such as Podesti, Gaetano Koch, Giuseppe Sacconi, and Manfredo Manfredi.[42] At the time he dedicated himself to the project for the National Stadium, the twenty-seven-year-old Piacentini was a successful young professional who had garnered many awards in important competitions and had a growing list of impressive private works.[43] Of special relevance to the stadium project was Piacentini's role as co-master-planner (with Gustavo Giovannoni) of the 1911 Exposition and designer of a number of its buildings.

In the press at the time, the new stadium design was described as a structure rising almost 10 meters above the ground which would have created "a sumptuous and pleasing backdrop to the grand setting in which it was placed."[44] The tiered seating was described as being below grade for two thirds of its height, while only the upper third rose above grade at the foot of the Parioli hill. The building, "with two long arms of tiered seats for the public, enclosed on one end by a semi-circle," was a reprise of the scheme of the *Kallimarmaro* even in its dimensions, excepting the greater width of the arena floor and the lesser height of the seating tiers, reduced "for aesthetic reasons." These descriptions largely conform to the drawings conserved in the Marcello Piacentini Archive in Florence, especially the bird's-eye perspective, in which the stadium is shown with the semi-circular end in the foreground [FIGURE 11].[45] The drawing shows the monotonous elevation of the part above ground marked only by rectangular windows and entrances to the spaces carved out below the seating; the tiers are uncovered and without a crowning portico.

The construction drawings for the National Stadium are conserved in the Archivio Storico Capitolino in Rome and bear the signatures of Piacentini and Guazzaroni. Examining them reveals how the building, while maintaining the plan shape of the previous solution, was made longer (220.20 meters) and wider (120.00 meters) in execution [Figure 12].[46] The load-bearing structure was formed by ninety reinforced concrete trusses[47] and the twenty-two rows of seats in concrete accommodated 23,000 persons, with an additional 3,000 places for standees on the uncovered promenade at the top. The plan was similar to that of Magni and Podesti at the Circus Maximus, although the latter was wider and two-and-a-half times longer. (As built, the National Stadium was 120 x 220 meters, while the proposal for the Circus Maximus was 140 x 620.) The new stadium was also smaller than the ancient Greek one, which in the times of Herod Atticus could seat 50,000 spectators in its forty-six tiers of seats, exactly double the number of tiers in the National Stadium.

The most characteristic element of the stadium was the entrance feature, for which Piacentini studied two alternatives. The first explored the solution visible in the aerial perspective, showing two massive lateral masses surmounted by tall pedestals and sculptural groups framing a hexastyle colonnade, above which runs a tall entablature with a modillion cornice [Figure 13]. The second study conforms to the elevation drawing in the construction documents [Figure 14].[48] Rejecting the more customary aspect of "a façade for a grand palazzo, all porticoes, windows, atria, arcades, and niches," Piacentini showed four columns engaged at each end by "square pillars upon which stand symbolic marble sculptural groups," preceded by stairs and two ramps for vehicular access.[49] The columns, linked at the top with a bronze frieze of festoons, shields, and garlands, were surmounted by representations of Fame (by the sculptors Angelo Barbieri and Romano Mazzini)[50] recalling both the *Rostra* of the Roman Forum and Piacentini's own design for the entrance to the Forum of the Regions

at the 1911 Exposition [Figure 15]. The choice of this decorative motif was a direct citation of the triumphal entrance of the athletes at the center of the open end in the structures built for similar spectacles in the Greek world.[51] Simultaneously at the Turin Exposition, freestanding columns bearing statues of winged victories decorated the monumental bridge of Valentino [Figure 16], while at the Rome Exposition the decorative program of the Forum of the Regions was curated by Giuseppe Guastalla, creator of the winged Victory placed on the column commemorating the breach of the Porta Pia.[52] Such classical citations assumed a widely-recognized patriotic and celebratory significance, linking contemporary Italy with its glorious imperial past [Figure 17].

Figure 11 (opposite top): M. Piacentini and V. Pardo, project for the National Stadium, Rome, 1908. Aerial perspective. (Biblioteca di Scienze Tecnologiche dell'Università di Firenze, Fondo Marcello Piacentini, filza 16.)

Figure 12 (opposite bottom): M. Piacentini and A. Guazzaroni, with the collaboration of V. Pardo, project for the National Stadium, Rome, 1910. Plan. (Archivio Storico Capitolino, Fondo Contratti, Atti Pubblici, 238, 7 dicembre 1911.)

Figure 13 (top left): M. Piacentini with the collaboration of V. Pardo, project for the National Stadium, Rome, 1908. First solution for the main entrance elevation. (Biblioteca di Scienze Tecnologiche dell'Università di Firenze, Fondo Marcello Piacentini, filza 16.)

Figure 14 (middle left): M. Piacentini with the collaboration of V. Pardo, project for the National Stadium, Rome, 1908. Second solution for the main entrance elevation. (Biblioteca di Scienze Tecnologiche dell'Università di Firenze, Fondo Marcello Piacentini, filza 16.)

Figure 15 (top right): M. Piacentini, Esposizione Etnografica, Foro delle Regioni, Rome, 1911. View of the entrance. (*Emporium*, n. 204, 1911, p. 415.)

Despite the claim that its "grandiosity was entirely Roman," the stadium was actually "inspired by the great Olympic stadium of Athens."[53] At the open end, a tetrastyle entrance feature similar to the second solution in the Florence drawings was built, except that the two lateral blocks became noticeably slenderer in execution. Such a solution was a further indication of the Greco-Roman "contamination" underlying the project, evoking the entrance of the *Kallimarmaro* of Herod Atticus, reconstructed in the Corinthian order for the "Intermediate

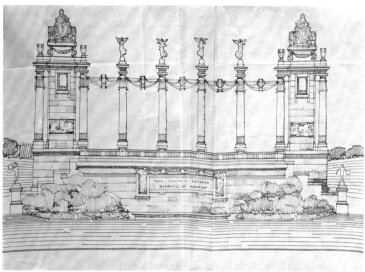

Figure 16 (top): Esposizione Internazionale dell'Industria e del Lavoro, Monumental bridge of Valentino, Turin, 1911. General view. (*Emporium,* n. 199, 1911, p. 43.)

Figure 17 (bottom): M. Piacentini and A. Guazzaroni, with the collaboration of V. Pardo, project for the National Stadium, Rome, 1910. Principal elevation of definitive design. (Archivio Storico Capitolino, Fondo Contratti, Atti Pubblici, 238, 7 dicembre 1911.)

Games" of 1906, while giving the stadium an architectural character decisively Roman in form and decoration [FIGURE 18]. In the end, the Rome stadium, like the one under construction at the same time in Turin, suffered cost-cutting simplifications of the original exterior design. The entire external elevation appeared extremely naked, replacing the originally-conceived decorative treatment with a sequence of simple openings revealing the structural frame. The contrast of these walls with the courtly entrance feature was rather sharp, even though this part, too, was simplified: The entrance was constructed without the designer's proposed ramps and the bases of the columns were brought down to grade level [FIGURE 19].[54]

On June 10, 1911 the new stadium was inaugurated in the presence of the King with an impressive ceremony involving hundreds of athletes and 1,500 schoolchildren. Thanks to the numerous areas planned for recreation and education below the stands, the new structure was hailed by the press as a true "house of physical education" in which the athletes would find an environment well-equipped for the cultivation of the mind as well as for engaging in sports.[55] But after the celebrations of the Roman Exposition the life of the National Stadium was cut short: Even though the structure could seat "only" 25,000 spectators (a third of the number in the contemporary stadium in Torino), the capacity was oversized with respect to the actual need at the time. In the following years, the building hosted a variety of events but fell progressively into disuse. With the coming of Fascism in 1922 there was a brief reprieve, and in 1927 ownership of the building was transferred to the National Fascist Party (PNF), whose officials decided to update it to reflect the party's sports policies, which sought to intensify the public sense of continuity with former imperial glories. The remodelling was again entrusted to Piacentini and Guazzaroni. On the inside of the arena they inserted a football pitch and installed a swimming pool, demolishing the former main entrance. They replaced this with a new screen of four massive columns linked by concave partition walls on a curved plan and surmounted by bronze statuary groups by the sculptor Amleto Cataldi representing Soccer, Racing, Wrestling, and Boxing[56] [FIGURE 20]. The seating capacity was increased to 30,000 spectators while the central tribune was covered by a reinforced concrete roof; in the curved end they carved out a two-story hotel to house the athletes. The renovated PNF Stadium, part of an extensive new sports zone consisting of hippodromes, soccer fields, and tennis courts, was officially inaugurated on March 25, 1928 followed by a match between the national soccer teams of Italy and Hungary.[57]

In subsequent years, the circus type reappeared in a series of stadium designs between 1912 and the 1930s, confirming the value of Amante's original proposal.[58] Wheras some of these modern stadiums de-emphasize the moral significance of the ancient classical models, pursuing instead designs based primarily on functional needs, the frequent use of the ancient plan configurations and a repertory of architectonic and ornamental elements traceable to their use in antiquity nevertheless recalls the types and features that enabled the spread of the circus and the amphitheatre throughout the Roman world.

In the post-war period, the building was once again threatened. After the airline disaster at Superga in 1949, the stadium was rededicated to the "Grande Torino,"[59] but shortly after that, in June 1955, the decision was taken by the International Olympic Committee to award Rome the XVII Olympic Games and this led to a move to replace the stadium with a new and more functional facility. The typological scheme of the stadium designed by Piacentini and Guazzaroni was too closely tied to the ideological premise inherent in the citation of the Panathenaic Stadium, considered as the cradle of "modern" sport. Besides, the architectural climate had also changed, and Italian post-war culture now looked to modernism and industrialism for emblems of national identity, unrelated to the symbols of continuity with the past that had served for three-quarters of a century. The Flaminio Stadium, designed by Pierluigi and Antonio Nervi, arose on the site of the PNF Stadium and was inaugurated in March 1959; its modernist form and reinforced concrete structure reveal an architectural conception altogether different from the designs of Amante, Piacentini, and the others [FIGURE 21].

THE NATIONAL STADIUM AND
CONTEMPORARY ROMAN ARCHITECTURE

To understand fully the importance of Piacentini and Guazzaroni's work at the Stadium we must bear in mind the decisive impact the 1911 Roman Exposition had on the entire Italian architectural community.[60] Piacentini had been named artistic director of the fair thanks to his close relationship with Mayor Ernesto Nathan but also, and above all, thanks to the international success he achieved the previous year with his Italian Pavilion at the Exposition in Brussels, in which we can identify a formal language similar to the fair buildings of 1911. The National Stadium was constructed along with the other exposition buildings, including the Gate of Honor and the Palace of the Fine Arts by Cesare Bazzani, one of the leading classical architects of the day [FIGURE 22], as well as the various international pavilions realized in the Valle Giulia, while the general exhibits were sited on the west bank of the Tiber across the new Ponte Flaminio designed in concrete by François Hennebique. Passing through the Gate of Honor, a work of Arnaldo Foschini and Ghino Venturi [FIGURE 23], one encountered the double exedra of Piacentini's Forum of the Regions, followed by the artificial lake and his Salon of the Festivities, flanked by the regional buildings. Here Piacentini employed a formal language recalling the sixteenth- and seventeenth-century architecture of Rome, particularly evident in the elliptical vestibule with a curved façade and freestanding columns of the Palace of the Festivities [FIGURE 24]. Nor was this an isolated case: The search for a durable connection with the classical culture of the past had prompted many explorations of the sixteenth-century style, as in the work of Guglielmo Calderini, for example, whose return to the lexicon of Sangallo and Michelangelo was animated by echoes of Piranesi to confer greater muscularity on a now-familiar *romanità* "rediscovered in modern times." [FIGURE 26].[61]

Despite considerable praise for his work, Piacentini was not satisfied with the outcome of the Exposition, with which he closed the first phase of his professional career. Even as the celebrations of the Fiftieth Anniversary were being set up, the debate about a national Italian style was once again in fashion.[62] Piacentini abandoned this search for a new style and finally addressed "modern" architecture,

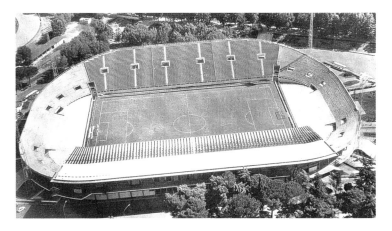

Figure 18 (Section opener, pages 6–7): M. Piacentini and A. Guazzaroni, with the collaboration of V. Pardo, project for the National Stadium, Rome, 1910. Aerial perspective. (Archivio Storico Capitolino, Fondo Contratti, Atti Pubblici, 238, 7 dicembre 1911.)

Figure 19 (top): M. Piacentini and A. Guazzaroni, with the collaboration of V. Pardo, National Stadium, Rome. Period photograph prior to the remodeling of 1927. (From Massari, S., ed., *La Festa delle Feste. Roma e l'Esposizione Internazionale del 1911*, Rome, Palombi editori, 2011, p. 170.)

Figure 20 (center): M. Piacentini and A. Guazzaroni, with the collaboration of V. Pardo, National Stadium, Rome. Period photograph after the remodeling of 1927 showing a detail of the entrance elevation. (Private collection.)

Figure 21 (bottom): Flaminio Stadium, designed by Pierluigi and Antonio Nervi and completed in 1959 on the site of the former National Stadium, Rome, aerial view. (Tummers, Tijs, D'Eletto, Clino, *Storia degli Stadi d'Italia illustrata da cartoline d'epoca*, Tesink, Zutphen, 2007, p. 127).

Figure 22 (top left): Cesare Bazzani, Esposizione Internazionale di Belle Arti, palazzo delle Belle Arti, Rome, 1911. View. (*Emporium*, n. 204, 1911, p. 408.)

Figure 23 (top right): A. Foschini e G., Venturi, Esposizione Etnografica, Gateway of Honor, Rome, 1911. View. (*Emporium*, n. 204, 1911, p. 409.)

Figure 24 (above): M. Piacentini, Esposizione Etnografica, Padiglione delle Feste, Rome, 1911. View. (From Massari, S., ed., *La Festa delle Feste. Roma e l'Esposizione Internazionale del 1911*, Rome, Palombi editori, 2011, p. 68.)

Figure 25 (left): M. Piacentini, Palazzo di Giustizia, Messina, 1912-28. View of principal elevation. (From Pisani, M., *Architetture di Marcello Piacentini. Le opere maestre*, Roma, Clear, 2004, p. 53.)

understood at that time as a return to unvarying classical principles.[63] In this sense, the aspiration to conjoin "Hellenic beauty" and "Roman permanence" underlying Piacentini's design for the National stadium was completely free of the "anxiety of renewal" that had marked the debate on a national style. The National Stadium appears, then, to be a precocious testimony to the interest nurtured by its author for the "Neo-roman Style" that would emerge more strongly in his work after the First World War, as at the Palace of Justice in Messina [FIGURE 25].[64] Piacentini's stadium project seems to recall the neoclassicism that came out of a conference held in Rome on 21 March 1901 sponsored by the Artistic Association of Architecture Enthusiasts (better known by its Italian name, the Associazione Artistica tra i Cultori di Architettura or AACA), which called for a balance between the monumental grace of the Greek and the composition of grand masses in the Roman building cultures.[65] What appeared to be a youthful intuition (Piacentini attended the conference even before completing high school)[66] developed further in the next phase of his career, during which he identified these values with *romanità:* an unerring formal code that he would later think appropriate to represent the city of Fascism. In the same period, other architects also adopted the poetics of grand and unadorned masses to express modernity, like Bazzani in his work of the Thirties. Both of these motives would characterize Piacentini's work in the following decades, part of a search for a "modern classicism" that extended far beyond Italy. Henry-Russell Hitchcock believed the early Piacentini, like Gunnar Asplund, was capable of simplifying the attempt to perpetuate the classical language that Auguste Perret and Peter Behrens had expressed in their work and, therefore, Piacentini came to be considered an "eclectic of neoclassical taste." In his solutions for the National Stadium, he drew freely on all the interpretations of Greek and Roman architecture but, as in other works of his early career, still rejected any break with the classical building tradition.[67]

To be precise, it should be stated that recourse to the formal code of classicism does not belong to the architecture of fascism, just as the architecture of fascism cannot be identified with the classical language. At least until the declaration of the Italian Empire in the mid-1930s, development of modernist architecture was not merely tolerated, but was even favored by the regime, as demonstrated by the work of designers like Luigi Moretti and Giuseppe Terragni, as well as numerous others in the major cities and the smaller towns.[68] The claim that classical architecture is indelibly stamped with a historical association with autocratic regimes disregards the full history of its use: It is true that during the Napoleonic Era the Arc de Triomphe in Paris (commissioned by Bonaparte and designed by Jean-François-Thérèse Chalgrin in 1806) and the Arco della Pace in Milan (begun the following year by Luigi Cagnola) were erected as symbols of the absolute power of the new Emperor; but a short time later in Germany, the same classical language was directed in opposition to French influence, as is apparent in the classical work of Karl Friedrich Schinkel in Berlin. For example, Schinkel's Schauspielhaus (1818-21) imposed a new character of severe rationality on its surroundings, laying the foundation for a coherent national architecture with a strong ideological stamp. The particular elaboration of the classical code in a "functional" key would make Schinkel one of the principal interpreters of "Germanness" in architecture.[69] In later periods, the classical language was adopted by other cultures that saw it as a means to express civil and democratic values, as in the United States.

In the case of Piacentini's National Stadium and the works realized for the Roman Exposition of 1911, reconnecting with the past had the value of a national expression. At the end of the nineteenth century, the search for a unified style for the new Italian state seemed to have focused its attention on a neo-Romanesque style. It was, therefore, not by chance that the buildings for the Exposition made reference not only to the architecture of ancient Rome, but to that of the Renaissance and baroque in order to identify an "absolute *romanità*" that would transcend strict chronological limits to embrace the full range of classicism since antiquity. At the very moment the city of Rome elected Ernesto Nathan mayor—a Mason from outside the nobility and un-beholden to the ecclesiastical power—Piacentini sought a difficult symbolic and architectural balance between the ancient and modern sources of classicism, with an objective very different from the one which he himself would pursue in his mature years during the fascist regime.[70]

The story of the National Stadium in Rome in the early twentieth century demonstrates, rather, the way in which historic types and the classical formal language were used to express different cultural and political contents. The wish to express architectural continuity between modernity and antiquity was paralleled by a desire to link the new Italy with its ancient forebears, even in the field of sports. This parallel was a consistent theme in Italian culture from at least the late nineteenth century until the end of the Second World War. While the relationship between the architect in the present and the architecture of the past can be both contested and fruitful, the tradition as a whole offers opportunities for the accommodation of new building tasks—as well as coherent expression of present-day aspirations—by means of a universally understood and continually evolving formal language. ✦

Raffaele Giannantonio is Adjunct Professor in the Department of Architecture at the Università degli Studi "G. d'Annunzio" at Chieti-Pescara, Italy, where he teaches architectural history. Among his recent publications are "Case ed Alloggi per impiegati in Piazza Caprera: Il contributo di Gustavo Giovannoni", in L'altra modernità nella cultura architettonica del XX secolo, Laura Marcucci (ed.), Rome: Gangemi Editore, 2012, La costruzione del regime. Urbanistica, architettura e politica nell'Abruzzo del fascismo, Lanciano: Carabba, 2006, and "Ellade e Roma": Lo Stadio Nazionale tra Giulio Magni e Marcello Piacentini, Pescara: Carsa, 2012.

Figure 26 (above): G. Calderini, Palazzo di Giustizia, Rome, 1887. Detail of final project. (From Accasto, G., Fraticelli, V., Nicolini, R., *L'architettura di Roma Capitale 1870-1970,* Roma, Edizioni Golem, 1971, p. 91.)

Notes

1. For histories in English of Italian architecture in the early twentieth century, see Kirk, Terry, *The Architecture of Modern Italy, vol. II, Visions of Utopia, 1900-Present*, New York: Princeton Architectural Press, 2005 and Meeks, C. L. V., *Italian Architecture 1750-1914*, London-New Haven: Yale University Press, 1966. For the cultural and political background of the 1911 Exposition, see Courtenay, Todd, "The 1911 International Exposition in Rome: Architecture, Archeology, and National Identity," *Journal of Historical Geography*, v. 37, 2011, pp. 440-459.

2. Capra, P., *Torino città di primati 333 volte prima in Italia*, Torino, Ed. Graphot, 2003.

3. Morasso, M., "Il programma sportivo dell'Esposizione di Torino," in G. Treves, Ed., *Le esposizioni del 1911: Roma, Torino, Firenze: rassegna illustrata delle mostre indette nelle tre capitali per solennizzare il cinquantenario del Regno d'Italia*, Milan: Fratelli Treves, 1911, p. 46.

4. Donghi, D., *Manuale dell'architetto*, Turin, Unione Tipografico-Editrice, 1924.

5. De Luca, P., "All'esposizione di Torino", in *Emporium*, XXXIV, December 1911, n. 199, p. 52.

6. *l Popolo Romano*, January 15, 1906.

7. The Stadium that hosted the Games in honor of the Goddess Athena was originally constructed with wooden seats, but in 329 BC, Lycurgus reconstructed it in Pentelikon marble. In 140 AD, Herod Atticus gave it a monumental form, increasing the seating capacity to 50,000 spectators. In this phase the structure measured 255 x 131 meters. The stadium remained buried and neglected for many centuries, but the prized marble was reused in other construction or burned for lime. The stadium was reconstructed in 1895 on the basis of the archeological finds by the architect Anastasios Metaxas in a manner faithful to the original design. The following year, the "new" stadium hosted the first edition of the modern Olympic Games, and was used again for some events in the Athens Games of 2004. See Gasparri, C., *Lo stadio panatenaico. Documenti e testimonianze per una riconsiderazione dell'edificio di Erode Attico*, Roma, L'erma di Bretschneider, 1978, Estratto da "Annuario della Scuola archeologica di Atene e delle missioni italiane in Oriente", 52,1974-75, pp. [313]-392).

8. See *Die Olympischen Spiele 776 v. Chr. - 1896 n. Chr., Mit Genehmigung und Unterstützung des Central-Comités der internationalen olympischen Spiele unter dem Vorsitze Seiner Kœnigl. Hoheit des Kronprinzen Constantin*, Athen, verlag von Carl Beck - Leipzig, F. Volckmar, London, H. Greveland Co, 1896.

9. Toschi, L., "Lo sport a Roma da porta Pia alla candidatura per le Olimpiadi del 1908", in *Studi Romani*, 3-4, November-December 1988 (XXXVI), pp. 311-324. On sport in Italy around the turn of the twentieth century, see Varrasi, F.M., *Economia, Politica e Sport in Italia (1925-1935). Spesa pubblica, organizzazioni sportive specializzate, impianti ed espansione delle pratiche agonistiche amatoriali e "professionistiche" in un paese a regime autoritario*, Graduate thesis of the Facoltà di Economia dell'Università degli Studi di Firenze, 1994-1995, p. 83-86; Fabrizio, F., *Storia dello sport in Italia. Dalle società ginnastiche all'associazionismo di massa*, Guaraldi, Firenze, 1978, p. 56-64; for other aspects cited in the text, see Croce, B., *Storia d'Europa nel secolo decimonono*, Laterza, Bari, 1932, 3 ed. Bari-Roma, 1972, p. 298-303; Rossi, L., "Sport e cultura operaia in Europa 1900-1939", in *Italia contemporanea*, September 1989, 176, p. 168-170; Turati, F., Discorsi parlamentari, Camera dei Deputati, Roma, 1950, vol. II, p. 856. On the relationship between sport, fascism, and Catholic associations, see Fabrizio, F. *Sport e fascismo. La politica sportiva del regime. 1924-1936*, Guaraldi, Firenze, 1977, p. 11-27 and Giannantonio, R., *La costruzione del regime. Urbanistica, architettura e politica nell'Abruzzo del fascismo*, Lanciano, Carabba, 2006, p. 476-495.

10. Amante, B., *L'educazione fisica in Italia nei rapporti con la scuola*, Roma, Cecchini, 1907.

11. Ibid., *Per il giubileo della Patria del MCMXI. Lo Stadio Nazionale nel Circo Massimo*, Roma, presso l'autore, 1908, p. 8.

12. "*Totam hodie Romam circus capit, et fragor aurem percutit, eventum "viridis" quo colligo panni*" (Juvenal, Satires, XI, 195). "All Rome flocks to the circus today, and a burst of applause greets the success of the green uniform."

13. Toschi, *Uno stadio per Roma …*, op. cit., p. 87n.

14. Legislatura XXII, 1a Sessione, Disegni e Relazioni, n. 617, p. 4, in *Progetto per lo Stadio Massimo Nazionale sull'area del Circo Massimo*, a cura di *Virides*, Federazione Scolastica Nazionale Educazione Fisica, Roma, Stabilimento Fratelli Capaccini, 1909, p. 21 and note 21.

15. Amante, *Per il giubileo …*, cit., p. 16.

16. The hippodrome in ancient Greek architecture was an open space served by tiered seating where horse races were held ("ippos" = horse, "dromos" = course). In Roman architecture, such races were held in the circuses, while the stadiums hosted athletic competitions, as in the Greek world. For an analysis of the typologies of the stadium and circus, see Gros, P., *L'architecture romaine, 1. Les monuments publics*, Paris, Picard editeur, 1996 and Humphrey, J., *Roman Circuses. Arenas for Chariot Racing*, University of California Press, Berkeley and Los Angeles 1986.

17. In the Greek cities, the ancient tradition of the equestrian contests was extremely different in character from the Roman *ludi circenses*. The structures consisted of tracks of beaten earth as in the hippodromes at Corinth and Athens. Only between the second and third centuries did hippodromes appear that reflected the monumental model of the Roman circus, but with different characteristics according to the province.

18. For the Latin terms, see notes 27 and 30. See also Gros, *L'architettura romana …*, op. cit., p. 396-397.

19. Gros, *L'architettura romana …*, op. cit., p. 398-399. Cfr. anche: Crema, L., "Architettura romana," in *Enciclopedia Classica*, XII, III, 1, Società editrice Internazionale, Torino, 1959, p. 207 sgg., 302 sgg. e 436 sgg.; Colini, A.M., *Stadium Domitiani*, R. Ist. di Studi Romani, Roma, 194; Akurgal, E., *Ancient Civilizations and Ruins of Turkey: from prehistoric times until the end of the Roman Empire*, Haset Kitabevi, Istanbul, 1973; Aupert, P., *Fouilles de Delphes, II. Topographie et architecture. Le stade*, En depot aux De Boccard, Paris, 1979; Welch, K., "Greek Stadia and Roman Spectacles: Asia, Athens, and the Tomb of Herodes Atticus", in *Journal of Roman Archaeology*, 11, 1998, 117-145; Aupert, P., "Evolution et Avatars d'une Forme Architecturale", in Landes C. ed., *Le Stade Romain et ses Spectacles catalogue de l'exposition, [du 4 juin au 20 octobre 1994]*, Lattès Musée archéologique Henri Prades, 1994, 95-106 ; Golden, M., *Sport in the Ancient World from A to Z*, Routledge, London, 2004.

20. Strabo, XIV, 639. The stadium at Laodicea, datable to 79 AD, also had short sides with a semi-circular plan. In addition to Azianoi and Ephesus, the stadium-theater type is also present at Perga and Aspendos.

21. See Suetonius, *Lives of the Caesars*, 39, 3, 7.

22. Gros, *L'architettura romana …*, op. cit., p. 400.

23. Among the structures of the type standing in Rome in the Imperial era, the Circus of Caligula and Nero was cited by Piny the Elder in *Naturalis Historia*, XXXVI, 74.

24. See Amante, *Per il giubileo …*, op. cit., pp. 20-21. He writes, "The stalls for the horses and chariots were arranged at the opposite end of the arena when viewed from the principal entrance of the Circus (the *porta triumphalis*). These stalls (called *carceres …*), were constituted by twelve *fornices* and a thirteenth in the center, where the *pompa circensis*—the solemn procession of the athletes—entered the field. (…) In the middle of the arena, running lengthwise, was a long raised berm *(spina)*, the truly sacred and monumental part of the circus because upon it was located the most prized mementos of the civil and religious history of the Romans: obelisks, aedicules, altars, columns, etc. The *meta* or *metæ*, conical constructions at the ends of the spina… were reminders of the etymology of the term circus which, beyond the meaning related directly to its form or the purpose it served, meant, according to Cassiodorus, Servius and others, only *circum enses*, because the *metæ* were trophies of weapons around which the chariots turned to make the drivers more artful and at the same time more meritorious in their triumphs. …(And) we must remember the *euripo*, which was the moat filled with water that separated the spectators from the arena to protect them from the wild animals. Julius Caesar constructed the euripo of the Circus Maximus, a canal 3 meters wide and equally deep to isolate the spectators (…) . Finally, *mæniana* (…) was an order of benches mounting up in concentric circles contained between two walkways that ran around the amphitheater and gave access to them. The *mœniana* was divided into a given number of equal sectors *(cunei)* by staircases *(scaltæ)* cutting them perpendicularly to allow the spectators to go up to their places."

25. Livy, I, 35,8-10. The *Trigarium* in the *Campus Martius*, the oldest space used for the training of race horses, was already in use during the Etruscan period and at the end of the Republican era it had acquired a rectangular plan arrangement with is southeast side arcaded.

26. To the west was located the *Ara Maxima* of Hercules near the Forum Boarium, and at the southwest were the temples of Ceres, Flora, Mercury, and Venus Obsequens.

27. In 329 BC, the *carceres* were constructed in painted wood on the curved side; toward the end of the 4th century BC the *spina* was arranged in the center of the track; in 196 BC, on the other short end Lucius Stertinius, upon his victorious return from Spain, constructed a triumphal arch *(fornix)* with gilded statues on top *(signa)*. (See Livy, *Ab Urbe condita,* 33, 27). In 174 BC, the censors Quintus Fulvio Flaccus and Aulus Postumius Albinus rebuilt the *carceres* in masonry, locating *metæ* at the ends of the *spina,* and at about the same time the rotating eggs were installed to indicate the number of laps to be completed. (Livy, XLI, 27, 6).

28. In 33 BC, to memorialize his naval successes, Agrippa placed on the *spina* the bronze dolphins that performed the same function as the eggs. The obelisk of Ramses erected by Augustus (now in the Piazza del Popolo) had come from Heliopolis in Egypt. The Imperial Box, more than the older *pulvinar,* seemed to resemble a sacred area dedicated to the gods presiding over the exhibitions. (Propertius, *Elegies,* II, 31).

29. Dionysus of Halicarnassus, *Roman Antiquities,* III, 68, 1-4. The Greek historian lived in Rome between 30 and 7 BC. In Canina's reconstruction, the total length was 640 meters and the width 235 meters, while the capacity was about 200,000 spectators.

30. The fire of 36 AD prompted the reconstruction in marble of the *carceres* and the installation of *metæ* in gilded bronze. The fire of 64 AD, which began right in the *cavea* of the structure, permitted Nero to rebuild it anew, bringing the capacity to 250,000 spectators. (Pliny, *Naturalis Historia,* XXXVI, 102). An umpteenth fire in the period of Domitian (started again in the wooden seats) gave rise to yet more modifications, the most important of which regarded the replacement by Titus of the *fornix* of Stertinius with a new triumphal entrance of three fornices. The curvilinear traces still visible of the substructures of the cavea erected between the Palatine and the Celio are attributed to the time of Trajan. This phase is documented in the famous marble map of Rome, the *Forma Urbis,* created in the period of Septimus Severus (203-211) and by a mosaic dated to the fifth century uncovered at the House of the Mosaics in Luni. (See Ciancio Rossetto, P., "Il nuovo frammento della Forma severiana relativo al Circo Massimo", in *Formae Urbis Romae. Nuovi frammenti di piante marmoree dallo scavo dei Fori Imperiali,* edited by R. Meneghini e R. Santangeli Valenzani, Roma, "L'erma" di Bretschneider, 2006, p. 127pp.)

31. Pliny the Younger, *Panegirico di Traiano,* 51, 2-5.

32. This had been pointed out in the eighteenth century: see Bianconi, G. L., *Descrizione dei circhi, particolarmente di quello di Caracalla e dei giuochi in essi celebrati,* a posthumous work in French edited by C. Fea, Roma, Paglierini, 1789 (cited in Amante, *Per il giubileo . . . ,* cit., p. 67).

33. Suetonius, *Cæsar,* XXX; Dio Cassius, LIII, 1º. The *quinquertium* originally included the long jump, footrace, wrestling, discus, and boxing. The modern version of the pentathlon was held for the first time in the fifth Olympic Games in Stockholm, 1912.

34. *La Tribuna,* 14 e 19 gennaio 1908.

35. *Progetto per lo Stadio Massimo Nazionale . . . ,* op. cit, p. 12 and 21. The Italian branch of *Audax* was a cycling association founded in 1898 by Vito Pardo in order to promote sport tourism.

36. The project for the National Stadium was the last project of Giulio Podesti (1857-1909). In his works, principally from the last quarter of the nineteenth century, he adopted a "moderate" classical language to satisfy the need for an urban and representative character in the new capital. (See Accasto, G., Fraticelli, V., Nicolini, R., *L'architettura di Roma Capitale 1870-1970,* Roma, Edizioni Golem, 1971, pp. 70-71, 138, 197.) In the same years, Giulio Magni was developing his practice in Rome, where he designed innovative public housing at Testaccio in 1905 and the complex for the Cooperative of Railroad Workers in Piazza Santa Croce in Gerusalemme, on which he was working when called to collaborate on the National Stadium. See Toschi, L., "L'edilizia popolare a Roma. Giulio Magni e il quartiere Testaccio", in *Avanti!,* 5 September, 1984, p. 9; Artibani, M., *Giulio Magni 1859-1930. Opere e progetti,* Roma: Edizioni Kappa, 1999, p. 65; Muratore, G., "Uno sperimentalismo eclettico", in *Storia dell'architettura italiana. Il primo Novecento,* op. cit., p. 30.

37. *Il Messaggero,* July 18, 1908.

38. *Progetto per lo Stadio Massimo Nazionale . . . ,* op. cit.

39. *Progetto di uno stadio in Roma,* in *L'Architettura Italiana,* v. IV, n. 7, April 1909, pp. 74-77.

40. Angelo Guazzaroni, at the time the head engineer of the municipal government of Rome, was born into a noble family in 1875 and had a career that continued until 1940. He was responsible for the realization of numerous public works, including the re-arrangement of the roadways and pedestrian access around the Coliseum (1939).

41. The publication produced by the Istituto Nazionale per l'Incremento dell'Educazione Fisica in Italia (INIEF) reported that the National Stadium had been designed based on the type of the Olympic Stadium of Athens. See *Stadio Nazionale in Roma,* Roma, Tip. Edit. Roma, 1910, [p. 1]).

42. Gaetano Koch (1849-1910) was among the most important architects in Rome after the city became the new capital of Italy. (See Pevsner, N., Fleming J., Honour, H., *A Dictionnary of Architecture,* London, Penguin Books, 1966). Giuseppe Sacconi (1854-1905) won the competition for the Monument to Vittorio Emanuele II (1884), whose work he directed until his death, after which it was completed in 1911 by Manfredi, Koch, and Pio Piacentini. (See Borsi, F., *L'architettura dell'Unità d'Italia.* Firenze, Casa Editrice Felice Le Monnier, 1966, parte IV, *I protagonisti,* cap. I, pp. 157-165; Meeks, C. L. V., *Italian Architecture 1750-1914,* London, New Haven, 1966, pp. 337-347). Manfredo Manfredi (1859-1927) designed and directed the construction of the new Ministry of the Interior on the Viminal hill (1911-26). (See Borsi F., Buscioni, M.C., *Manfredi Manfredi e il classicismo della nuova Italia,* Milano, Electa, 1983; Gigli, L., "Manfredo Manfredi", in *Il Vittoriano. Materiali per una storia,* II, Roma, Fratelli Palombi, 1988, pp. 151 s.).

43. In the first part of his long and fortunate career, Marcello Piacentini (1881-1960) participated in important competitions and designed residences for affluent Romans. In 1906 he won the competition to remodel the center of Bergamo. In 1908 he obtained the commission for the National Stadium as well as the master plan for the proposed 1911 Exposition. After the First World War he dominated official architecture in Italy, and was responsible for directing the most important state projects. (See Pisani, M., *Architetture di Marcello Piacentini. Le opere maestre,* Roma, Clear, 2004, pp. 22, 23; De Rose, A.S., *Marcello Piacentini. Opere 1903-1906,* Modena, Franco Cosimo Panini, 1995, p. 28, 107).

44. This and the following citations are from *Il Messaggero,* February 26, 1909; *Progetto di uno stadio in Roma,* op. cit.; *Stadio Nazionale in Roma,* op. cit.

45. The drawings are conserved in the Biblioteca di Scienze Tecnologiche dell'Università di Firenze, Fondo Marcello Piacentini, filza 16.

46. *Lo Stadio a Roma,* op. cit.

47. Giorino, *Lo Stadio di Roma inaugurato,* cit., p. 210.

48. In the same folder is another drawing that represents a long colonnaded elevation closed at the sides by two triumphal arches, also colonnaded, probably an additional solution for the entry feature.

49. *Il Messaggero,* 26 febbraio 1909.

50. Angelini, L., "I palazzi e gli edifici delle Esposizione di Roma. Valle Giulia e Piazza d'Armi," in *Emporium,* XXXIV, dicembre 1911, n. 204, p. 418.

51. Varrasi, *Economia, Politica e Sport . . . ,* op. cit., p. 219.

52. See Paroli, L., Baldinotti, S., "Foro delle Regioni," in *La Festa delle Feste. Roma e l'Esposizione Internazionale del 1911,* edited by S. Massari, Roma, Palombi editori, 2011, p. 63. On 20 September 1870, the Italian army besieging Rome managed to breach the Aurelian Walls near the Porta Pia. In this way the city was stormed and delivered to the new unified State, and the following year became the official capital, succeeding Turin and Florence.

53. Giorino, *Lo Stadio di Roma inaugurato,* op. cit., p. 210.

54. Baldinotti, S., "Stadio Flaminio", in *La Festa delle Feste . . . ,* op. cit., p. 170.

55. *Progetto di uno stadio in Roma,* op. cit., p. 77.

56. *Il Messaggero,* August 11, 1929.

57. On June 10, 1945, the Stadium was the site of the finals of the second edition of the world soccer championship, won by Italy over Czechoslovakia.

58. Stadiums with conspicuous displays of classical architecture and sculpture of antique inspiration were constructed in numerous countries in the following decade, from Rome's Stadio dei marmi (Enrico Del Debbio, 1928) to Chicago's Soldier Field (Holabird and Roche, 1924): the second had the same U-shaped configuration as the stadiums proposed for Rome in 1911.

59. On May 4, 1949, the airplane bringing home almost all of the champion Turin soccer team crashed into the hill below the Basilica of Superga, outside Turin, killing all aboard. The tragic loss of the team, popularly known as "Grande Torino," deeply affected the Italian public.

60. On this subject, see *La Festa delle Feste . . .* op. cit., and Courtenay, op. cit.

61. Muratore, *Uno sperimentalismo eclettico*, op. cit., pp. 20-21.

62. Bossaglia, R., "Dopo il Liberty: considerazioni sull'eclettismo di ritorno e il filone dell'architettura fantastica in Italia," in *Scritti in onore di Giulio Carlo Argan*, Roma, Multigrafica, 1984-85, p. 213.

63. Lupano, M., *Marcello Piacentini*, Laterza, Roma, 1991, p. 17. Arianna Sara De Rose associates the fascination with Roman imperial architecture in Piacentini's buildings with the contemporary scenographies for epic films set in ancient Rome, like "The Last Days of Pompeii" (1908) and "Spartacus" (1909). The close relation between film and architecture, then and now, deserves further study. See De Rose, *Marcello Piacentini . . .*, op. cit., p. X. A return to a more sober Romanism in civic architecture was also the dominant trend in the United States, as evidenced by the work of McKim, Mead & White during the same years.

64. Pisani, *Architetture di Marcello Piacentini . . .*, op. cit., p. 45.

65. Piacentini, M., *Lo stile neo-classico e la sua applicazione in Italia*, Roma, Tumminelli, [1901?]

66. Ibid., "Confidenze di un architetto. Marcello Piacentini," in *Scienza e tecnica*, vol. 7, February 1943, fasc. 2, pp. 56-57. Piacentini attended courses in architecture at the Istituto romano di Belle Arti, where in 1906 he received a diploma as professor of drawing. In 1912 he obtained his degree in civil architecture at the Scuola di applicazione degli ingegneri in Rome, based on a Regio Decreto issued *ad personam*. (See Lupano, Marcello Piacentini . . ., cit., pp. 4-5).

67. Hitchcock, H.R., *Architecture Nineteenth and Twentieth Centuries*, London, Penguin Books, 1958, p. 534.

68. On Italian architecture between the world wars and the relationship between the large cities and the smaller towns, see the Giannantonio, *La costruzione del regime . . .*, op. cit.

69. Middleton R., Watkin D., *Neoclassical and 19yh Century Architecture*, Harry N. Abrams, New York, 1976, (Italian edition., *Architettura dell'Ottocento*, Electa, Milano, 1977), p. 267-268. On neo-classical architecture, see Mellinghoff T., *German Architecture and the Classical Ideal*, MIT Press, Cambridge Mass., Thames & Hudson, London, 1987. On the architecture of the Age of Enlightenment, the classic text remains Kaufmann, E., *Architecture in the Age of Reason*, Cambridge, Harvard University Press, 1955.

70. On the figure of Marcello Piacentini see also the recently-published book, Ciucci, Giorgio, S. Lux, and F. Purini, eds., *Marcello Piacentini architetto 1881-1960*, Roma, Gangemi Editore, 2012. Mayor Ernesto Nathan was elected in 1907 and re-elected in 1911. His administration was notable for attempts to regulate the intense building development throughout the city and to promote the construction of humane social housing.

Acknowledgements: The author wishes to thank Steven Semes, Luisa Boccia, and Assen Assenov for their assistance with translations for this article.

Academic Portfolio

Academy of Classical Design

By D. Jeffrey Mims

As sometimes happens in life, many years may pass before we recognize the significance a single moment can have for our future. For me, such a moment was the Arthur Ross Awards ceremony on May 7, 1984 at the National Academy of Design in New York. Having just turned thirty, and in the august company of accomplished classicists, I was to receive an award for my fresco work in North Carolina. This ceremony, only the second since its inception, was held before the great mural study for the Minnesota State Capitol building painted by the American artist Edwin Howland Blashfield.

This image was familiar to me through having read a 1913 edition of his *Mural Painting in America*, which seemed to hold historical secrets from an ancient past, inspired with an optimism that was to be checked the following year by the outbreak of World War I. Presiding over this ceremony was Henry Hope Reed, Jr., President of Classical America and one of its founders. Reed had been born right after the first year of that terrible war and had begun his life during the waning years of the American Renaissance. During his long life, he witnessed the twentieth century's "secession" (as he so aptly labeled it) from the beauty and logic of our classical heritage; fittingly, he was destined to become the leading champion of its restoration.

After returning home, I ordered a copy of Reed's *The Golden City*, which introduced me to his revolutionary ideas, articulated for me

the purpose of mural painting, and confirmed the earlier emphasis by Blashfield on its role as part of a larger ensemble that included architecture, sculpture, and landscape. I had dimly felt this sense of overall design in beautiful civic spaces in my earlier travels, but learning the fundamentals of traditional painting had been such a struggle in those days that understanding its employment in a broader context was a great discovery.

Now thirty years later, encouraging advances have been made by a small band of determined artists to recover the nearly lost art of figure drawing and painting; however, very little attention has been given to what Reed considered to be its ultimate application —the decoration of architectural space through mural painting, particularly in the public realm. Considered in this context, the figure is one of many design elements used to orchestrate the decoration of an architectural space, joined in this task by painted borders, geometric patterns, cartouches, festoons, and other ornamental devices. But where can these be studied today? It is our emphasis on traditional mural painting that distinguishes the Academy of Classical Design from the growing number of studio schools dedicated to a renewal of the fine arts. The Academy, which began as Mims Studios in 2000, traces its philosophy at least as far back as that auspicious evening in 1984 when I was introduced to Reed and his vision of the allied arts—a vision of built environments that please, inspire, and leave us with a sense of wonder.

To achieve this purpose requires a profound knowledge of "the classical" and the many variations within that heritage—a requirement involving no small amount of time or patience—and this is the first lesson taught to our students at the Academy. In the tradition of Renaissance workshops and the art academies that evolved from them, our curriculum devotes a great deal of time to the very thing modern art education has taught us to avoid—copying. For us, copying has three primary goals: The first is to gain a rich visual vocabulary; the second two are closely related—to develop recognition of excellence

Figure 1 (Section opener, pages 36-37): Academy of Classical Design. Students Allison Sexton and Olena Babak at work on paintings from plaster casts of antique statuary, 2013. Photograph courtesy of the Academy of Classical Design.

Figure 2 (opposite top): Academy of Classical Design. Student Peter Daniel working on underpainting a section of a mural copy from Raphael's ceiling tondo "Justice" at the Stanza della Segnatura, The Vatican, oil on panel, 96" x 120", 2013. Photograph courtesy of the Academy of Classical Design.

Figure 3 (opposite left): Academy of Classical Design. "Cast Drawing of the Torso Belvedere in The Vatican," charcoal on white paper, 32" x 22", 2013, by Peter Daniel.

Figure 4 (opposite right): Academy of Classical Design. "Life Drawing," charcoal and white chalk on toned paper, 27" x 38", 2013, by Olena Babak.

Figure 5 (following page): Academy of Classical Design. "Acanthus Relief," 26" x 31", graphite and watercolor on toned paper, 2013, by Allison Sexton.

decoration. Unique to our program is what we call the Mural Guild, which allows advanced students the opportunity to produce full scale painted copies from acknowledged masterworks. Each of these studies contributes to the development of the taste and ability necessary for future work of a more collaborative nature.

Unlike many other art schools, working from life and the model enters our program only after a profound study of the role it has played in the history of drawing, sculpture, and painting. Such a departure from usual practice is based on historical precedent, as well as the need to counteract a contemporary abandonment of the traditional use of the human figure. Each student begins with a series of two-dimensional copies from the nineteenth-century drawing course of Charles Bargue, taught using a translation developed specifically for our curriculum. From the very start, emphasis is placed on mastering the skills needed to imitate nature as beautifully and as intelligently as possible. Considerations of time are never allowed to interfere with quality: A project may take from one week to several months, depending on a number of factors.

Growing awareness of the role of the painter in architecture has brought an increase not only of public interest but also of knowledgeable partners to collaborate *with*—including patrons, architects, artists, and artisans. Henry Hope Reed's argument for beautiful public spaces embellished through the allied arts becomes ever more convincing as we see how the barren modern alternative has affected the quality of our lives. The growing number of committed people working toward a renewal of "the classical" is testimony to the success of his life's mission, which continues to give direction to so many.

D. Jeffrey Mims is founder and director of the Academy of Classical Design in Southern Pines, North Carolina, a non-profit school of art dedicated to the classical tradition with an emphasis on public mural painting. Mr. Mims is the recipient of an Arthur Ross Award in 1984 and the ICAA 2009 Alma Schapiro Prize for an affiliated fellowship at the American Academy in Rome. For more information see www.academyof classicaldesign.org

as well as the ability to recognize its opposite. Two other components within these goals are the imitation of nature and familiarity with the historical uses of that ability. The oscillation between realism and idealism found in Greek sculpture is a stylistic conversation with a variety of accents that continued into the twentieth century. For the mural painter, the ability to idealize forms and generalize effect is crucial for the successful decoration of architectural spaces; but to reach that point one must first be a humble student of nature. More accurately, I should say nature guided by antiquity, because in learning to manage a credible likeness, there are also lessons to be absorbed indirectly through working with the masterful conventions of Greek form.

Meticulous plaster cast work is augmented with assignments that reach beyond the mysteries of illusion, such as the making of compositional and color studies from different periods in the history of Art, as well as the study of anatomy and pure ornament. A basic architectural vocabulary is introduced as it relates to classical interiors that have traditionally made use of painted and sculpted

RIEGER-GRAHAM PRIZE
2012–2013

WINNER:
Daniel Heath

PROJECT: "The Rome of Alexander VII"
In 2012, Daniel Heath was awarded the Rieger-Graham Prize, a biennial three-month affiliated fellowship at the American Academy in Rome given by the Institute of Classical Architecture & Art (ICAA). The subject of his study was the architectural and urban interventions of Pope Alexander VII (reigned 1655-1667) under the design direction of Baroque masters Gianlorenzo Bernini, Francesco Borromini, and Pietro da Cortona, among others.

The product of his research was a drawing composed as a cartographic and pictorial survey of the works undertaken in Rome during the Pope's reign. The center of the presentation is a map based on the Map of Rome of Giambattista Nolli (1748) locating the projects sponsored by the pontiff, accompanied by views of the Scala Regia in the Vatican Palace by Bernini; the pair of domed churches at the Piazza del Popolo by Bernini, Carlo Rainaldi, and Carlo Fontana; and the Piazza della Pace by Da Cortona. Born Fabio Chigi in 1599, Alexander VII had perhaps the greatest impact on the physical form of Rome of any of the popes. His projects of diverse type and scope shared an architectural and urbanistic vision characterized by the term *teatro*, or urban theater. Daniel Heath's graphic study locates these varied projects within a comprehensive vision of the city as a model for urban embellishment and decorum.

Figure 1 (right): "Cortile in the McKim Building, American Academy in Rome," graphite and watercolor on paper, 17 3/4" x 11 3/4", 2013.

Front Endpapers: "The Rome of Alexander VII," graphite on paper, 39 ¾" x 66", 2013, by Daniel Heath.

Back Endpapers: Detail, "The Rome of Alexander VII," graphite on paper, 39 ¾" x 66", 2013, by Daniel Heath.

THE BEAUX-ARTS ATELIER, INSTITUTE OF CLASSICAL ARCHITECTURE & ART

STUDENTS:
Seth Baum, Corey Strange, Abigail Tulis.

INSTRUCTORS:
Richard Cameron
Michael Djordjevitch

PROJECT: An Equestrian Monument to George Washington, New York, 2013
The pinnacle of the ICAA's educational program is a one-year intensive study of classical architecture at the Beaux-Arts Atelier in New York. In the class of 2012-13's design studio, students turned their attention to one man and one monument: The man was George Washington and the monument a 1906 bronze sculpture depicting Washington leading his troops through the fierce winter of 1777-78 at Valley Forge. The bronze sculpture was the work of Henry Mervin Shrady, creator of the Ulysses S. Grant Memorial on the West Front of the United States Capitol in Washington, D.C. His statue of Washington was placed atop an imposing granite base at the center of Continental Army Plaza, the former Brooklyn approach to the Williamsburg Bridge over the East River. Once a heraldic civic gesture, the statue of Washington is now largely forgotten, even defaced, and the plaza is forlorn.

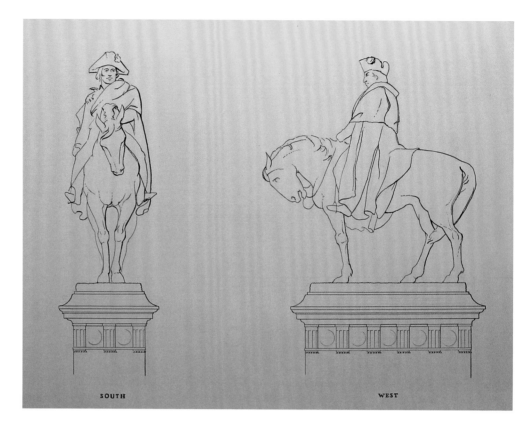

SOUTH   WEST

Students were asked to study proposals for relocating the Shrady sculpture to a more notable location—on the Bowling Green in Lower Manhattan, in front of Cass Gilbert's monumental Custom House—atop a base of their own design. The project began with measured drawings of the existing statue and base in its present location. A series of design studies were then made, culminating in an *analytique* showing the statue and its new base in its new location. The assignment is both a design project and a history project: a sketch of history as understood by those just beginning to explore the classical language of architecture, with the aim of making this history a part of the living present.

Figure 1 (top): Equestrian Monument to George Washington. Measured drawing of existing monument, 2013. The statue is by Abigail Tulis and the base of the statue is by Seth Baum.

Figure 2 (left): Equestrian Monument to George Washington. Preliminary sketch of proposed design, 2013 by Corey Strange.

Figure 3 (opposite): Equestrian Monument to George Washington. Analytique of completed design, 2013 by Corey Strange.

JUDSON UNIVERSITY
Master of Architecture program
Spring 2013

STUDENT:
Andrew Gander

INSTRUCTORS:
Christopher Miller
Ian Hoffman
James Gray

PROJECT: Smithsonian Institution Archives Building, Washington, D.C.

This proposed civic building is part of a reimagined southwest district of Washington, D.C. An archives building typically serves to safeguard and conserve a collection of documents. Not simply a vault, the Smithsonian Institution Archives Building also acts as a public educational center. A grand reading room is open to the public for research and review of the collection. A gallery for rotating exhibitions promotes awareness of the holdings of the Institution and provides an opportunity to showcase particular pieces to the public. The event hall hosts receptions, lectures, and other special events. The facility preserves documents in its conservation laboratories and a digitization studio, which gives the collection new life in the digital world.

Figure 1 (left): Perspective view of Reading Room by Andrew Gander, 2013.

Figure 2 (above): Perspective view of exterior by Andrew Gander, 2013.

HAMPTON UNIVERSITY
Department of Architecture Study Abroad Program in Europe, 2012-2013

STUDENTS:

Design Team: Darrel Alexander, Christopher Armstrong, Alicia Canady, Uri Cooper II, Nicole Downs, Alexis Hayes, Trevor Jones, Chace Kea, Quince McCurley, Willie Parks, Maressa Pinnock, Alisonya Poole, Zachary Robinson, Isha Somerville, Meredith Stone, William Wanzer.

INSTRUCTORS:
Mason Andrews
Ray Gindroz

Hampton University is a historically black university founded after the Civil War to train newly emancipated African-Americans for productive lives as middle-class citizens. Its Department of Architecture has for many years included a travel program which sends students to Asia, South America, Africa, and Europe. Over the years, faculty members participating in the program have included Shannon and David Chance, Ron Kloster, and Department Chair Robert Easter. Recently, the three-week travel has focused on urban studies followed by an urban design studio on campus in which students develop proposals for a site in one of the cities visited. Participating students have completed the first three years of the five-and-a-half-year Master of Architecture degree.

Since 2009, many of the students have worked with Ray Gindroz, FAIA, in France and Italy to examine Leon Battista Alberti's suggestion that a well-crafted city is like a house in which the streets are corridors and the *piazze* are urban rooms. These studies have two didactic foci: observation and documentation through sketching and measured drawings to understand how buildings conspire to create successful urban spaces, and conversations with local political leaders and design professionals in the cities studied. These conversations provide opportunities for students to learn of the perceptions and aspirations of community members and suggest that their own professional futures might involve shaping not only individual buildings but neighborhoods, cities, and regions. The faculty finds that returning students have undergone a shift in their own sense of their futures and their discipline: They have learned to listen and to look in a new way, their skills and efforts are turned to working on something larger than shiny objects made to impress, and they have learned the dance of collaboration—both in architecture and in life.

During the years 2011–13, the itinerary in France included Aix-en-Provence, Nîmes, Marseille, Uzès, Toulon, and Paris, with design projects sited in Toulon. The travel programs have been underwritten in part by the Sol Cohen Fund and through the generous support of the Marilyn and Ray Gindroz Foundation and Daryl and Robert Davis.

Figure 1 (top): 2013 Design Project: New entry to the Old City, Toulon. The team project proposes redevelopment of the roof of an existing parking structure to create a new entrance to the historic center. On the left is new development, including the bell tower, with the seventeenth-century *corderie* on the right. Perspective view. Rendering by Chace Kea.

Figure 2 (bottom): 2013 Design Project: New entry to the Old City, Toulon. Another view showing the pedestrian street lined with residential buildings. Perspective view. Rendering by Chace Kea.

UNIVERSITY OF COLORADO DENVER

Master of Architecture program
Spring 2013

STUDENT:
Sean McMurray

INSTRUCTOR:
Cameron Kruger

PROJECT: A House on a Corner Lot
This single-family house by a third-year graduate student is located on a corner lot along one of Denver's landmark parkways inspired by the City Beautiful Movement. The site is across from Cheesman Park and among houses by Jacques Benedict and Fisher & Fisher, two of Denver's best firms in the 1920s and 30s. In this context, the solution to the program is both restrained and elegant, and the massing is straightforward. Most of the program is contained within a single rectangular volume, with a conservatory off the study that suggests a whimsical addition. The garage separates the front yard from the more relaxed back yard and its detailing is more restrained than that on the principal volume.

Much of the interest of the scheme lies in the careful axial planning. While the wide range of room shapes and sizes demanded by the program led to an asymmetrical composition, the designer successfully wove the rooms together by the axial placement of door and window openings. The internal disposition of rooms is evident on the façade facing the Parkway, with its asymmetrical arrangement informed by the work of Hawksmoor and Lutyens. Of similar inspiration is the rusticated Doric order visible in the *analytique*.

Sean McMurray is one of the first class at the University of Colorado Denver to complete the new "Atelier" advanced studio course. Students may take this studio only after first completing the elective course in classical architecture, which covers the five orders, shadow casting, and ink wash rendering. Students may also continue their classical studies and, upon completing the required history, theory, and drawing classes, earn a certificate from the ICAA.

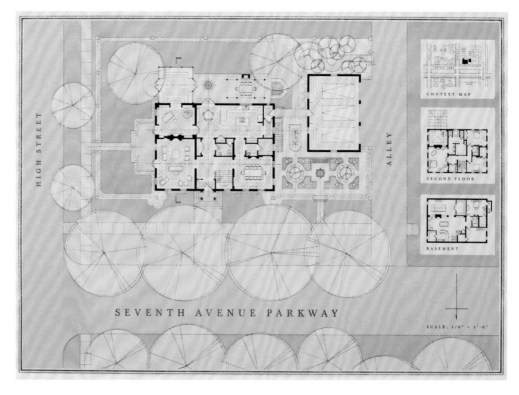

Figure 1 (top): A House on a Corner Lot, Denver, Colorado. Street façade, 2013 by Sean McMurray.

Figure 2 (bottom.): A House on a Corner Lot, Denver, Colorado. Floor plans 2013 by Sean McMurray.

Figure 3 (opposite): A House on a Corner Lot, Denver, Colorado. Analytique, 2013 by Sean McMurray.

1828 EAST SEVENTH AVENUE PARKW

ENTRANCE

UNIVERSITY OF NOTRE DAME

First Year Graduate Design Studio
Fall 2012

STUDENTS:
James Paul Hayes
Reynaldo Hernandez

INSTRUCTOR:
Steven Semes

PROJECT: An Academy of the Decorative Arts, Chicago, Illinois

The Academy of the Decorative Arts was conceived as a school and exhibition center for training in and showcasing of the decorative arts, specifically those associated with traditional architecture and its ornament and decoration. The program included a public exhibition gallery, library, and bookstore, plus studios for drawing, painting, sculpture, and ornament. The corner site is at Huron and Rush Streets on the North Side of Chicago, adjacent to the Murphy Memorial, the Driehaus Museum, and St. James Episcopal Cathedral. Students were encouraged to explore the types of the Italian palazzo and the French *hôtel particulier* and their possible adaptation for the program. The requirements of the project were intentionally kept simple to allow students to concentrate on the architectural development of the building and its ornament and decoration. This was the first major project of the introductory course in classical architecture for students who entered the graduate program with previous degrees in architecture.

The two projects shown here indicate the range of exploration: Ray Hernandez's project remained largely faithful to the palazzo type in plan and volume, with a glazed *cortile* rather than an open-air courtyard; abundant ornament and decoration of Italian Renaissance inspiration enlivens the exterior. Paul Hayes investigated a formal language derived from Parisian work at the turn of the twentieth century, including both classical and art nouveau elements.

A DECORATIVE ARTS ACADEMY
CHICAGO, ILLINOIS

Figure 1 (top): Academy of Decorative Art, Chicago. Perspective view and site plan, 2012 by Reynaldo Hernandez.

Figure 2 (above): Plan of ground floor, 2012 by Reynaldo Hernandez.

Figure 3 (left): Exterior details, 2012 by Reynaldo Hernandez.

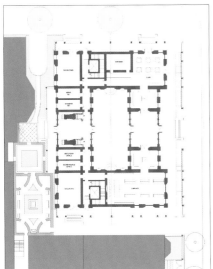

Figure 4 (top): East Elevation, 2012 by James Paul Hayes.

Figure 5 (far left): Ground floor plan, 2012 by James Paul Hayes.

Figure 6 (left): Section looking west, 2012 by James Paul Hayes.

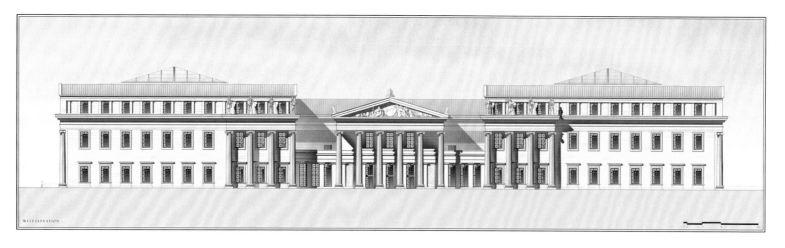

UNIVERSITY OF NOTRE DAME

Fifth Year Undergraduate Thesis
Spring 2013

Students:
Elizabeth Kelley
Julian Murphy

Instructor:
David Mayernik

Project: A Counter-proposal for the Humboldt Forum, Berlin

For their thesis projects, Elizabeth Kelley and Julian Murphy presented a counter-proposal to Franco Stella's competition-winning design for the Humboldt Forum, the new art and culture complex to be constructed on the site of the former Stadtschloss, or city palace, in the center of Berlin. The palace, former residence of the Prussian kings and German emperors, was partially destroyed by bombing in World War II and finally demolished by the East German government in 1950. Since the re-unification of Germany after 1989, the site has been marked by dispute over its future. Stella proposes the reconstruction of three façades of the palace around a modern interior, despite changes in programmatic and urban functions.

The counter-proposal pursues the restoration of the building's original values rather than recreating its former appearance. Because the original palace was not celebrated primarily for its artistic or architectural

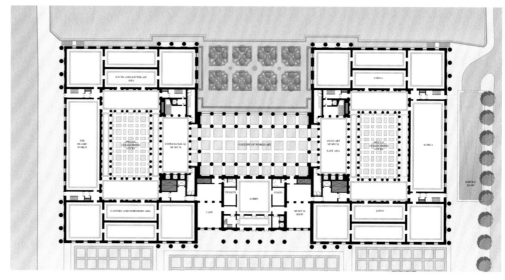

significance but, rather, for its important role in shaping the urban fabric of the city center, the students proposed a new cultural forum that formally expresses its role as museum, events center, library, and performance venue, while maintaining the historic importance of the site and reinforcing its role as a civic hub in the center of Berlin. The program for the Forum was divided among four buildings: an entrance "Agora," a library, a museum, and a performing arts hall. The Forum's classical character emulates the nineteenth-century German neo-classicism of Schinkel, Langhans, Gilly, Gentz, and others as represented in Berlin's most beloved monuments, while also referencing their sources in ancient Greece.

Elizabeth Kelley designed the Non-European Museum, divided into two distinct collections—an Ethnological collection and one devoted to Asian Art—disposed in two separate wings. A grand central hall, which serves as a Gallery of World Art, links the two wings and their collections. The galleries are arranged *enfilade* around sky-lit courts. Each wing has its own vertical circulation, allowing the collections to be visited independently. The Ionic order is drawn from the temple of Athena at Priene, an ancient non-European site, fittingly used here to indicate the museum's Non-European art. Sculptural decoration is used internally and externally to further represent the collections housed in the museum.

Julian Murphy designed the performing arts center, including a 350-seat lecture hall and a 500-seat multi-purpose auditorium. These are disposed symmetrically about a central spine passing through the building

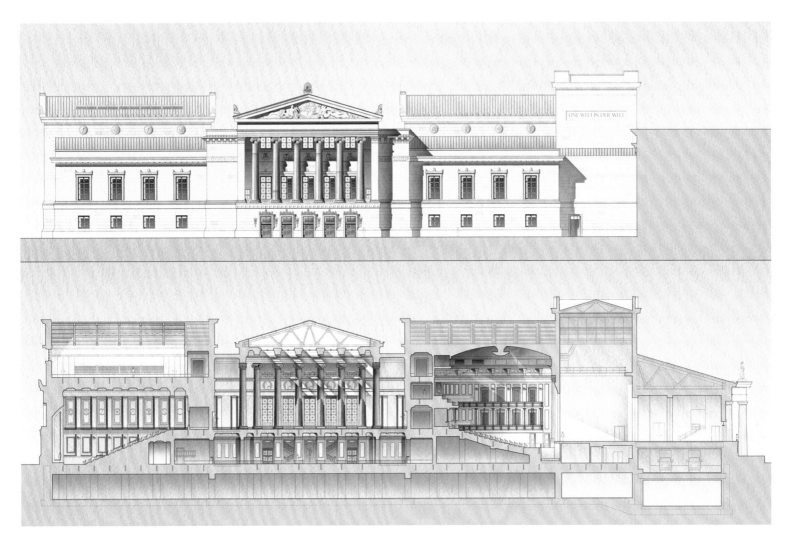

and consisting of a sequence that moves from a grand foyer where a skylit upper lobby is visible, through a low entrance hall with ticketing and coatrooms, and up a grand staircase to the skylit double-height shared lobby. The secondary functions—seminar rooms, a café, offices, etc.—are located north and south of the main event spaces, allowing both main facades to have windows. A *scaenae frons* on the west façade both masks a necessarily windowless elevation and provides the backdrop for an outdoor theater with seating for over 300.

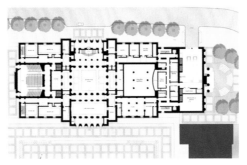

Figure 1 (opposite top): Museum of Non-European Art, Humboldt Forum, Berlin. Front elevation, 2013 by Elizabeth Kelley.

Figure 2 (opposite bottom): Museum of Non-European Art, Humboldt Forum, Berlin. Main floor plan, 2013 by Elizabeth Kelley.

Figure 3 (top): Performing Arts Center, Humboldt Forum, Berlin. Main elevation and longitudinal section, 2013 by Julian Murphy.

Figure 4 (above left): Performing Arts Center, Humboldt Forum, Berlin. Main floor plan, 2013 by Julian Murphy.

Figure 5 (above right): Performing Arts Center, Humboldt Forum, Berlin. West elevation, 2013 by Julian Murphy.

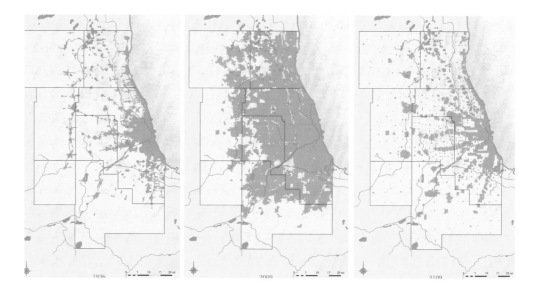

UNIVERSITY OF NOTRE DAME

The University of Notre Dame Graduate Urban Design Studios, 2011-12

STUDENTS:
Daniel Acevedo, Bryce Buckley, William Gay, Sam Lima, Diana (Reising) Dempsey, Andy Rutz, Arti (Waghray) Harchekar, Hannah Weber (Fall 2011), Michael Geller, Michael Mabaquiaio, Ian Manire, Brian Mork, Stacey Philliber, Jennifer Pope, Joel VanderWeele (Fall 2012)

INSTRUCTORS:
Philip Bess and Douglas Duany, *Instructors*
Jennifer Griffin and John Griffin, *Visiting Research Assistant Professors*
Will Dowdy, *Research Assistant*

PROJECT: The Notre Dame Plan of Chicago 2109
On July 4, 1909, at a moment when Chicago was both the fastest growing and most quintessentially modern city in the world, the Commercial Club of Chicago published Daniel Burnham and Edward Bennett's Plan of Chicago. Justly praised to this day for its ambition, its regional scope, and its environmental prescience, it is also often criticized for its ambition as well as its alleged autocratic social and design sensibilities. Less commonly noted is that the Plan of Chicago was one of the last attempts to employ classical principles of architectural, landscape, and urban design in, for, and at the scale of a rapidly expanding modern industrial metropolis; and it did this consciously participating in Western culture's long tradition of classical humanist urbanism. Nevertheless, in its centennial year of 2009, most commentators treated the Plan of Chicago as a noteworthy historical document the substantive relevance of which has passed.

Against this latter assessment, and with a different set of assumptions about human nature, architecture and urbanism, as well as a different view of where contemporary culture is moving, the University of Notre Dame graduate urban design studio undertook a two-year study of Chicago *in media res* that projects the city forward to 2109, the bicentennial of Burnham's 1909 Plan. Intended in part to critique, update, and improve the original plan, but even more to critique what present-day Chicago has become, our study asks: What might a modern metropolis be like if it were designed from within a tradition of classical humanism informed by Catholic sacramental sensibility and a biblical understanding of Man as an intermediate being both part of and accountable for nature? Taking the Plan of Chicago as a starting point and Chicago as a test case, The Notre Dame Plan of Chicago 2109 proposes that classical architecture and urbanism and modern Catholic social teaching can help locate the modern metropolis in both nature and sacred order in ways both symbolically legible and humane.

The 2109 Plan projects forward, and presumes—indeed requires—continuous but different cultural and economic conditions than those now prevailing. More precisely, the Plan is premised upon a narrative of cultural and environmental transformation: a story of decline and revival, in which an oil- and automobile-dependent global economy and an individualist therapeutic culture, both of which found their primary material expression in suburban sprawl and hyper-modern architecture, proved demographically, environmentally, economically, and culturally unsustainable, and were required to reassess and recalibrate. The conjecture of the 2109 Plan is that the original Plan of Chicago, locally sustainable agricultural and industrial economies, traditional materials and methods of construction, and communal religious traditions (including Catholic intellectual culture and social teaching), will be part of that recalibration. So too is the hope that—even if for economic reasons we will be more place-based and less mobile—we will be a more humane, just, beautiful, environmentally sustainable and spiritually substantive culture than we are now.

Like the 1909 Burnham Plan, The Notre Dame Plan of Chicago 2109 entails architecture, urban design, and planning at a metropolitan scale. Anticipating a period of regional economic and population decline, the Plan seeks to help restore and enhance environmental, economic, and cultural sustainability in metropolitan Chicago by means of good land use, good transportation policy, good building practices, and good urban form. Expecting the gradual decay and abandonment of post-1945 suburban sprawl development primarily for demographic and infrastructure cost reasons, the 2109 Plan envisions the reclamation of some 70% of metropolitan Chicago's urban footprint as open land for agriculture, commercial forestry, passive waste-water treatment, forest preserves and prairie. Combined with a re-reversal of the late nineteenth-century reversal of the Chicago River and the creation of new regional active (city) and passive (town and country) water treatment districts, these changes will also help restore regional aquifers and send more water back to the Great Lakes Watershed.

The 2109 Plan proposes to re-urbanize in-city interstate rights-of-way, and to re-establish a regional urban–agrarian culture across a range of settlements—from Hamlets to Villages to Towns to Cities—with agricultural activities, population density, and land coverage appropriate to each. The Plan envisions a polycentric metropolis of urban neighborhoods and towns located along existing and extended city and regional commuter rail lines; proposes to enhance metropolitan Chicago's commercial environment by means of simple form-based zoning codes subservient to local community-developed master plans; and depicts a public realm of parks, plazas, squares, avenues, boulevards, and streets established as normative and beautiful spaces belonging to all.

At the center of the 2109 Plan is a proposal to reclaim the current Chicago Circle freeway interchange and re-imagine the original Plan of Chicago Civic Center proposal for this site: specifically, by restoring its east-west civic axis terminating on a new high-rise City Hall at Congress and Halsted, and by adding a north-south cross-axis fronted by sacred buildings. This new axis would acknowledge the sacred dimension and orientation of human culture generally and the founding principles of the United States in particular; it also offers a critique of contemporary commercial-bureaucratic-therapeutic culture and its prevailing urban form. The result is both traditional and new, informed by anthropology and historical precedent, but distinctively American and unique to Chicago. The 2109 Plan expresses the formal implications of America's constitutional mandate of religious non-establishment and free exercise, as well as the reality of America's religious pluralism, by making the sacred axis a free and clear boulevard-cum-mall defined and fronted by blocks of mixed-use background buildings punctuated by sacred foreground buildings of different religious communities (including non-Christians).

Although we hope our project's multiple ambitions will resonate with people everywhere, including the professional and academic community, we acknowledge that the 2109 Plan challenges both the modernist and the hyper-modernist narratives that prevail in the contemporary culture of architecture and urbanism. We at Notre Dame welcome ensuing conversation, believing that the broad classical humanist tradition we are striving to re-learn, teach, and extend possesses ample resources to address contemporary society's most demanding architectural and urban formal problems. More controversially perhaps, the

Figure 1 (opposite): Metropolitan Chicago Land Use drawings show 2109 neighborhood and town development along city and commuter rail lines. The 2109 Plan reclaims as farmland, forest and prairie 70% of the land occupied by sprawl in 2009, and reverts to historic pre-1945 patterns of human settlement.

Figure 2 (below): An aerial view toward the west depicts a city of neighborhoods and parks, and a region of transit-oriented towns in a natural and agrarian landscape.

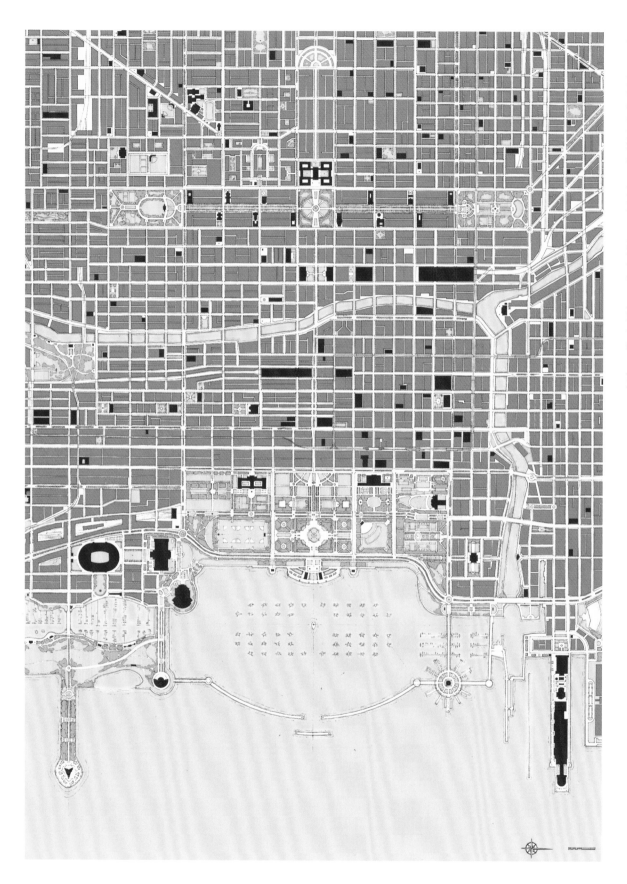

Figure 3 (left): Within the constraints of re-purposed existing infrastructure rights-of-way, the proposed plan for the historic center shows a recovery and extension of Burnham's baroque-scale civic intentions, an expansion of Chicago's public parks, and a proliferation of neighborhood-scaled squares and civic buildings.

Figure 4 (opposite top): Notre Dame Plan of Chicago 2109. Perspective view of Sacred Axis, looking north.

Figure 5 (opposite left): Notre Dame Plan of Chicago 2109. Perspective view of proposed new high-rise City Hall at Congress and Halsted.

Figure 6 (opposite right): Notre Dame Plan of Chicago 2109. Perspective view of the "Crossing" of the Civic and Sacred Axes, looking northwest.

All drawings courtesy of The University of Notre Dame Graduate Urban Design Studio.

2109 Plan also challenges secularist paradigms in the culture at large. Modernity is the proximate source of many genuine goods and we should all be grateful for them; but all genuine goods are grounded in God. Many at Notre Dame believe our well-being, both communal and individual, requires us to acknowledge this, not least in the way we make our buildings and cities.
—*Philip Bess*

Financial support for The Notre Dame Plan of Chicago 2109 has been provided by The Historical Society (Boston, Massachusetts) as part of its two-year multi-disciplinary research project Religion and Innovation in Human Affairs.

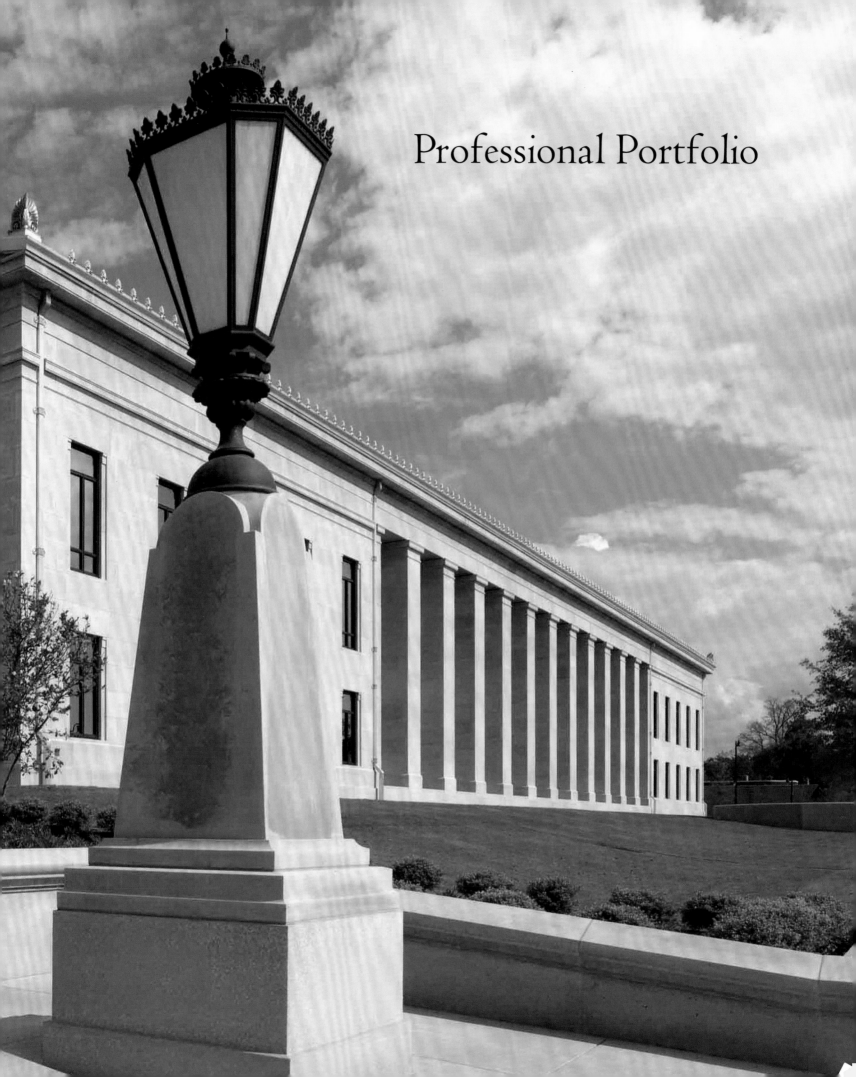

Professional Portfolio

HBRA Architects

Chicago, Illinois

The Richard H. Driehaus Prize, 2013

United States Federal Building and Courthouse
Tuscaloosa, Alabama

Project Team:
Thomas H. Beeby, Aric Lasher, Dennis E. Rupert, and Craig Brandt, *Project Principals*

The United States Federal Building and Courthouse, completed in 2011, is a 127,000 square foot facility housing a diverse range of federal tenants while accommodating the enhanced security, circulation, and infrastructure needs of the U. S. District and Bankruptcy Courts components. The building establishes a dignified presence for the federal government and provides a civic resource for the city of Tuscaloosa by expressing the cultural legacy and aspirations of the region through carefully considered planning, building systems and technologies, architectural vocabulary, and an artistic program that expands the building's role as a shared cultural resource for the area's citizens.

The Federal Building is placed on a landscaped platform that allows it to satisfy perimeter security requirements while maintaining an open appearance. Internal components are arranged around an enclosed central atrium that runs the length of the long axis of the building. This space is the primary circulation spine and is illuminated from above by clerestory windows, affording easy orientation for building users and visitors.

The building meets both LEED and EPACT energy conservation requirements, achieving a LEED Gold certification. The use of regional architectural and landscape materials, durable building systems, and a timeless architectural expression all support the building's commitment to sustainability and the responsible assignment of resources.

Figure 1 (Section opener, pages 56-57): U.S. Federal Building and Courthouse, Tuscaloosa, Alabama. View of main entrance. Photograph by Timothy Hursley.

Figure 2 (below): U.S. Federal Building and Courthouse, Tuscaloosa, Alabama. View of entry elevation. Photograph by Timothy Hursley.

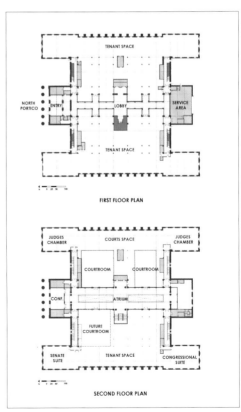

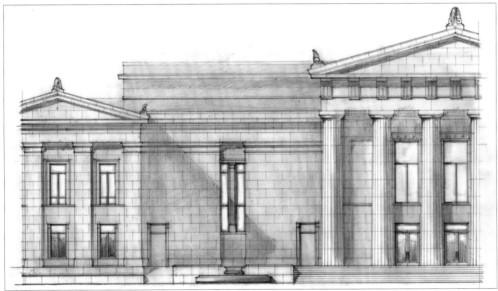

Figure 3 (top left): View of atrium. Photograph by Timothy Hursley.

Figure 4 (top right): Preliminary sketch of atrium. Drawing by Aric Lasher, HBRA Architects, Inc.

Figure 5 (above left): Design drawing of exterior. Drawing by Aric Lasher, HBRA Architects, Inc.

Figure 6 (right): Floor plans. Courtesy HBRA Architects, Inc.

Fairfax & Sammons Architects

New York, New York

ARTHUR ROSS AWARD FOR
ARCHITECTURE, 2013

PROJECT TEAM:
Anne Fairfax, *Principal*
Richard Sammons, *Principal*

The 2013 Arthur Ross Award was presented to Fairfax & Sammons Architects, PC in recognition of their achievement over the two decades since their office was founded in 1992. The firm's international practice specializes in private residential projects, but its forays into the public realm and urban design have also garnered acclaim. The partners, Anne Fairfax and Richard Sammons, are among the leaders of their generation of classical architects, having had remarkable success in balancing professional practice, scholarship, teaching, and leadership roles in several cultural institutions. Their projects have been widely recognized for their beauty of conception, detail, and craftsmanship, and have been published frequently in the design press, as well as in the monograph *American Houses: The Architecture of Fairfax & Sammons* (Rizzoli, 2006). The firm maintains offices in New York and Palm Beach, Florida.

Sammons' longtime interest in the classical theory and practice of proportion is evident in all the firm's work, as well as in his teaching and contributions to ICAA publications, including the forthcoming *Classical Architecture: A Handbook to the Tradition.* He has taught at the ICAA, the University of Notre Dame, Pratt Institute, the Prince's Institute, and the Georgia Institute of Technology. Both partners are longtime supporters of Classical America and the ICAA, Sammons having been among the original founders of the Institute of Classical Architecture in 1991. Fairfax served as Chair of the Board 2006-09. In addition, the partners are members of the International College of Traditional Practitioners, The Attingham

Trust, The Royal Oak Society, and have served on the Architectural Review Commission and the Landmarks Commission of Palm Beach, Florida.

In addition to the Arthur Ross Award, the firm has received Charter Awards from the Congress of the New Urbanism, Philip Trammell Shutze Awards from the Southeast Chapter of the ICAA, Addison Mizner Awards from the South Florida Chapter of the ICAA, the Stanford White Award of the ICAA, the 2013 Hyland Award for Excellence in Architecture, the Three Sisters Award, and the National Trust for Historic Preservation award in Interior Design. Their work has also been recognized by the Municipal Arts Society of New York and the Greenwich Village Society for Historic Preservation, among others.

Figure 1 (above): Urban Design and New Hotel for Marion Square, Charleston, South Carolina (2008). Perspective view. Part of a charrette sponsored by neighborhood groups to provide a positive model for future development of the area on the north side of Charleston's historic district, the plan seeks to define the square and reinforce important vistas by adding mixed-use buildings, better managing traffic and parking, and enlivening pedestrian life. A new hotel, designed by the firm in association with Goff D'Antonio Architects, is now under construction. The master-plan for the Marion Square received a Charter Award from the Congress for the New Urbanism in 2009.

Figures 2 and 3 (opposite): Urban Design for the Historic Center of Andorra (2009). An urban intervention in the capital of Andorra in the Pyrenees, the program included a new 32,000 square foot building for the Universitat d'Andorra, a new parking structure, and 79,000 square feet of mixed residential, retail and office space, as presented in another architect's scheme which had proposed demolition of the area. Fairfax & Sammons proposed restoration of three existing nineteenth-century buildings and a new "Propylea" to maintain the historic Plaça Major, while providing pedestrian access to a new square enclosed by new buildings continuing the architectural types and language of the historic center. The project received a Charter Award from the Congress for the New Urbanism in 2010.

Figure 4 (top): New Marina Housing, Albany, The Bahamas (2008). Elevation facing marina. This resort community comprises 565 oceanfront acres on the island of New Providence. Opened in early 2010, buildings were commissioned from a number of leading international architects. The firm's mixed-use buildings integrate indoor and outdoor living spaces and offer views of the marina, ocean and golf course.

Figure 5 (above): Regency House Renovation, Palm Beach, Florida (2000). View of living room. The Hans Fischer residence was built in 1970 to the design of John L. Volk, a prominent traditional architect in Palm Beach of the time. Fairfax & Sammons remodeled the entire building but maintained the essence of Volk's butterfly plan. The exterior was given a more classical treatment and the interior was completely refitted, creating a series of grand reception rooms. Mlinaric, Henry & Zervudachi were the interior decorators and Charles Stick designed the gardens. Photograph by Durston Saylor.

Figure 6 (opposite right): New Federal-style House, Cooperstown, New York (2003). View of portico. Farmlands, as this house is called, is a rural retreat conceived in the manner of earlier country houses, with a hierarchy of spaces and functions, traditional architectural language, and strong relationship to the landscape. The pair of Palladian windows in round-arched recesses framing vistas from the dining room and library recall the designs of Federal-period architects like Latrobe and Bulfinch. Photograph by Durston Saylor.

Figure 7 (top left): Greenwich Village Townhouse Restoration, New York (2013). Fairfax & Sammons is known for its restoration of period houses, such as this complete interior refurbishment of a nineteenth-century townhouse, including interior decoration. View of living room toward fireplace. Photograph by Durston Saylor.

Figure 8 (top right): Greenwich Village Townhouse Restoration, New York (2013). A view of the doorway and into the stair hall, where the stair was rebuilt using an original salvaged mahogany newel post from a demolished house in the neighborhood. Photograph by Durston Saylor.

Figure 9 (right): Greenwich Village Townhouse Restoration, New York (2013). A detail of the door case and its cornice. New classical detailing in the interiors recreated what had been lost over the previous century. Photograph by Durston Saylor.

Ferguson and Shamamian Architects

New York, New York

Stanford White Award for
Residential New Construction, 2012

Private Residence
Westport, Connecticut

Located on a large waterfront site on the Long Island Sound, this 16,000 square foot project includes a new main house, new pool and pool house, new sunken tennis court and tennis pavilion, and the renovation of existing buildings for use as a guest house and garages. With a central hall plan, clapboard exterior, and rich architectural details inspired by British eighteenth-century pattern books, the house recalls Colonial-era houses of New England.

On the main floor, a large living room, oak-paneled library, dining room, bar, and sitting room provide ample space for entertaining. The butler's pantry off the dining room leads to a large family kitchen with fireplace and adjoining family room. At the main stair landing, a Serliana window frames a window seat overlooking the motor court, gardens and tennis pavilion; at the second floor landing, a sitting room overlooks the rear lawn and Long Island Sound. All of the bedrooms and the master suite are on the second floor. The third floor includes three large game rooms accessed by two stairs and entered through archways in the two massive chimneys. A theater, bar, gymnasium, and service rooms occupy the basement level. Extensive new gardens and landscaping complete the exterior program.

Figure 1 (right): Private Residence, Westport, Connecticut. Construction details of front entrance. Courtesy of Ferguson Shamamian Architects.

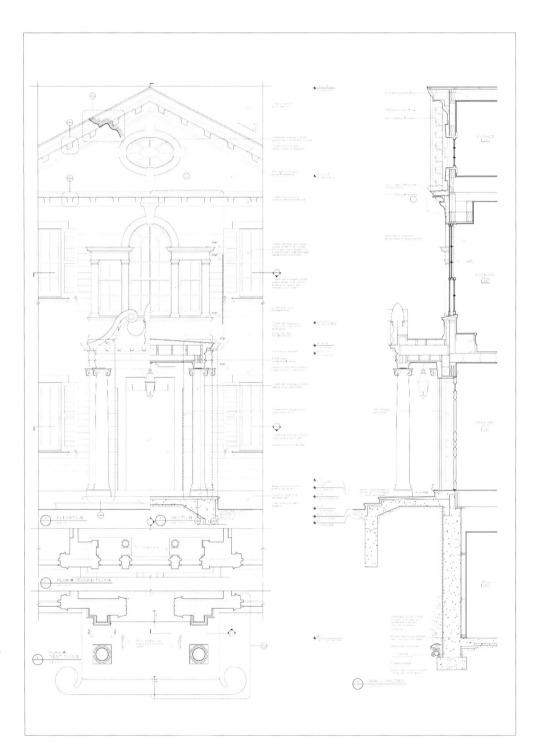

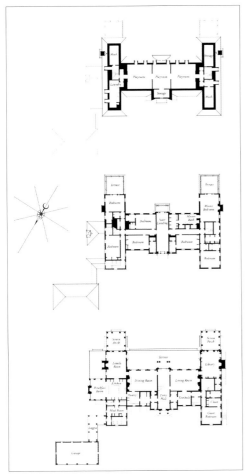

Figure 2 (top left): Private Residence, Westport, Connecticut. Overall view of main entry. Photograph by Scott Frances.

Figure 3 (top right): Private Residence, Westport, Connecticut. Detail of main entry. Photograph by Scott Frances.

Figure 4 (left): Private Residence, Westport, Connecticut. Floor plans. Courtesy of Ferguson Shamamian Architects.

Figure 5 (above): Private Residence, Westport, Connecticut. View of stair hall. Photograph by Scott Frances.

Krier · Kohl Architects

Berlin, Germany

Brandevoort Housing, Block 18
Helmond, Netherlands, 2009

Project Team:
Rob Krier and Christoph Kohl, *Principals*
Frank Altpeter and Dominque Krämer, Erik Aarts
Architect, Helmond, Netherlands, *Associated Architect*

The new town of Brandevoort has been under development since 1996 for about 17,000 inhabitants on a 365-hectare site between Eindhoven and Helmond in the Dutch province of Brabant. The urban plan is based on the principles of a traditional Brabant city. The city center, or Veste, is the relatively densely built-up urban core, surrounded by several outer quarters consisting of around 4,400 detached and semi-detached houses. The design of the center is inspired by traditional urban spatial compositions and is shaped by an old country road in an east-west direction and an elongated market square with a canal flowing in a north-south direction. Apart from approximately 1,600 dwellings in town houses and apartment buildings, the Veste contains a railway station, market hall, shops, cafés and restaurants, a health center, and schools.

Block 18 is located adjacent to the Hertogsveld, a tree-filled public space in the western part of the Veste. Addressing this green square are spacious urban row houses of four stories. Parking is provided by garages

constructed behind the ground floor of the houses. The garage roofs are terraces and spacious private gardens extend to the back of the lot. The side streets are predominantly lined with row houses of two stories with taller houses on the corners. Natural stone and brick are integrated in the façades of the individual houses, giving them a distinctive and authentic character.

On the initiative of the developer Kalliste, students of the University of Notre Dame School of Architecture's Rome Studies Program were involved in the preliminary designs of block 18 in 2007. The students in Ettore Maria Mazzola's studio developed hand-drawn designs for the individual houses. These preliminary designs constituted the basis for the developed design work.

Figure 1 (left): Block 18 Housing, Brandevoort, Helmond, Netherlands. Urban plan. Drawing courtesy of KK Urbanism-Architecture-Landscape.

Figure 2 (top): Drawing by Kaitlin O'Brien, University of Notre Dame, April 2007.

Figure 3 (above): View of completed houses. Photograph by Patrick Pagel (Archives KK Urbanism-Architecture-Landscape).

Ettore Maria Mazzola

Rome, Italy

Urban Regeneration of a Suburban District
Corviale, Rome, 2010

This project proposes to replace the most emblematic and controversial modernist housing project in Rome: the complex at Corviale, designed by Mario Fiorentino and completed in 1982. The existing structure, a social and stylistic descendant of the Unité d'Habitation of Le Corbusier, is a "ground-scraper" one kilometer long intended to house nearly 6,500 inhabitants, and has long been noted as an example of failed modernist public housing programs. It is also viewed by many Romans as a blight on the landscape of the city's south-western suburbs. The proposal replaces the existing mega-structure with a human-scaled new traditional district in a manner that is both economically feasible and specifically phased to avoid dislocating the current residents, who will be able to remain in the new community. An additional 2,000 residents will also be accommodated, along with new shops and businesses to create a complete social and economic community.

The new Borgo Corviale recovers all pre-existing infrastructure (such as sewers, aqueduct, gas, and electric utilities, etc.) and the layout of pre-existing streets is largely recovered and completed. Vehicular access is provided to all the buildings, pedestrian accessibility inside the village is guaranteed, and the edges of the district are carefully defined. The walk along the central pedestrian spine is punctuated by five piazzas, creating a promising environment for the commercial activities on the ground floor of the buildings. The neighborhood also includes a post office, church, town-hall, local police station, and a school complex. The existing library/cultural center is relocated to one of the new piazzas. Public and private parking lots are provided, including ground-

level on-street parking and structured parking underneath the buildings and the piazzas. Finally, the whole built space of Corviale would be surrounded by a great park.

The project received an International Design Award from the 49th International Making Cities Livable Conference in Portland, Oregon in 2010. The jury noted that the project "provides an exemplary model for urban renewal throughout the world."

Figure 1 (top): The New Borgo Corviale. Perspective view of piazza with parish church. Drawing by Ettore Maria Mazzola.

Figure 2 (right middle): Top: Corviale Housing Project, Rome, Italy, by Mario Fiorentino and others, completed 1982. Aerial view of existing conditions. Photograph courtesy of Immagine TerraItalyTM by Pictometry – © Compagnia Generale Ripreseaeree.

Figure 3 (right bottom): The New Borgo Corviale. Proposed urban design plan. Drawing by Ettore Maria Mazzola.

The Prince's Foundation for Building Community

London, England

THE PRINCE'S NATURAL HOUSE

2011

PROJECT TEAM:
Ben Bolgar, *Project Director*
Lenka Schulzova, *Project Manager*
Michael Romero, *Project Manager*
Kingerlee Construction, *Builder*

The Prince's Natural House is a demonstration project traditionally built from natural materials and its energy-efficient design does not rely on gadgets or hi-technology to make it "green." The sponsors' intention was to show ordinary people how simple choices can lead to lower-impact, more natural, and healthier homes. The House was designed to conserve energy in its construction and be cost-effective to maintain. The walls are clay blocks with lime-plaster rendering, a naturally-insulating system, and the roof is insulated with sheep's wool and wood fiber, making the house warm in winter and cool in summer, with reduced household utility bills.

Family health was another factor in the design, in contrast with many "eco-homes" that do not consider interior air quality—especially important with asthma on the rise. The Natural House uses breathable materials, including paints and floor finishes, so that dust and moisture are not trapped and able to cause damp or mold. Principles of sustainability ought to apply to interior design as well as architecture. Project interior designer, Christina Moore, used recycled materials, including curtains and bedspreads made from a patchwork of found materials from market stalls or items destined to be discarded, proving that good design need not be expensive.

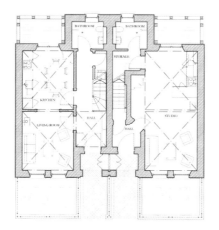

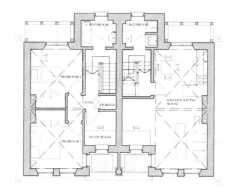

Figure 1 (top): The Prince's Natural House. View of completed house. Photograph by Richard Ivey.

Figure 2 (middle left): Ground floor plan. Courtesy The Prince's Foundation for Building Community.

Figure 3 (middle right): Upper floor plan. Courtesy The Prince's Foundation for Building Community.

Figure 4 (right): View of entry hall. Photograph by Richard Ivey.

Luigi Del Sordo Atelier di Ingegneria ed Architettura Urbana

Alba Adriatica, Italy

QUARTIERE BIANCOSPINO
Alba Adriatica, Italy, 2008

PROJECT TEAM:
Michelangelo D'Errico, Sabrina Palazzese, Fabrizio Parnanzone, and Fabrizio Puccinotti

"Il Biancospino" is a new neighborhood for social housing, consisting of 153 apartments, 7 ground-floor shops, and 12,000 square meters of public space, including a central pedestrian piazza and a 4,000 square-meter public garden. Situated in the immediate vicinity of the town center of Alba Adriatica, it has been designed according to the principles of traditional urbanism, with streets, squares, and urban blocks harmoniously composed to stimulate the social lives of the inhabitants and integrate with the existing urban fabric in the surrounding areas. The preliminary design phase benefited from the collaboration of students from the Rome Studies Program of the University of Notre Dame School of Architecture.

Within the constraints of current zoning regulations, the center and boundaries of intervention are clearly defined, providing greater complexity in the urban composition with several new connections to the existing street network. The urban blocks are smaller near the center, with high building density and commercial spaces to ensure the vitality of the public square and pedestrian paths; they are instead more extensive near the boundaries of the quarter, presenting smaller buildings limited in height and enclosing small gardens. There is also a new public garden enjoyed by all citizens of the district; its form and location is dictated by the need to preserve an important view towards the hills and create a symbolic union with the landscape.

Figure 1 (above): Quartiere Biancospino, Alba Adriatica, Italy. View from the landscape.

Figure 2 (bottom left): Quartiere Biancospino, Alba Adriatica, Italy. Aerial view.

Figure 3 (bottom right): Quartiere Biancospino, Alba Adriatica, Italy. View into central courtyard.

All images courtesy of Luigi Del Sordo Atelier di Ingegneria ed Architettura Urbana.

George Saumarez Smith of ADAM Architecture

London, England

Richard Green Gallery
London, England, 2011

This new building in the Mayfair Conservation Area of the City of Westminster replaces two unlisted structures on the site from the nineteenth and early twentieth centuries, both of which had been degraded by previous remodeling. The built façade in Portland stone is of demonstrably higher quality than the pre-existing buildings; this was important to persuade local authorities that well-designed and well-executed new construction can make a more positive contribution to the historic character of the area than retaining pre-existing, but compromised façades. The architect further suggested that the new front include sculpture, as there is a strong tradition of architectural decoration in Bond Street and throughout the Mayfair Conservation Area. Sculptural reliefs by Alexander Stoddart in the spandrels between the second and third floor windows depict the Legend of the Winnowing Fan from Homer's Odyssey—a metaphor for the creative quest of the artist.

The architect, one of the "Three Classicists" (together with Francis Terry and Ben Pentreath) whose 2010 exhibition at the Royal Institute of British Architects in London showcased these leaders of a new generation of classical designers in the United Kingdom, notes "the architecture and the sculpture led each other down quite a formal neo-classical route...but my intention was that the design should also have a definite modernity to it and not be mistaken for an old building." The project received the Georgian Group's 2011 Giles Worsley Award for New Building in a Georgian Context.

Figure 1 (right): Richard Green Gallery, 33 New Bond Street, London. View of façade. Photograph by Morley von Sternberg.

John Simpson Architects LLP

London, England

KENSINGTON PALACE LOGGIA
London, England, 2012

PROJECT TEAM:
Hockley & Dawson, *Structural Engineer*
Ramboll (formerly Giffords), *Services Engineer*
Chris Topp & Co., *Architectural Metalwork*
Nimbus, *Stone Mason*

The architects' 2008 master plan sought to facilitate access to portions of Kensington Palace open to the public, while much of the structure remains a residence for the Royal Family. The project provides a new entrance on the eastern side and reconnects the palace with its gardens and adjacent Hyde Park. The new cast iron and glass loggia creates a recognizable public entrance for the first time and enhances the legibility of the existing elements of the palace.

The Regency-inspired design for the cast iron frame incorporates acroterions and anthemions, in reference to the garden, as well as The Queen's cipher and the date 2012 in celebration of Her Majesty's Diamond Jubilee. The glass of the elegant pendant lights is engraved with the same motifs. Gilded ropes and tassels, also cast in iron, complete the festive appearance.

In accordance with conservation requirements, the loggia does not impact the historic fabric, from which it is structurally independent, and the installation is fully reversible. Local conservation authorities initially objected that the loggia "might be mistaken for something that had always been there." Working closely with English Heritage and other advisory groups, the design team finally received all necessary approvals and the addition was completed in 2012.

Figures 1 and 2 (top): Kensington Palace Loggia, London. Exterior and interior details of the loggia.

Figure 3 (bottom): Restored east façade and loggia.

All Photographs by Andreas von Einsiedel / John Simpson Architects LLP.

Todd Furgason

Fayetteville, Arkansas

Pi Beta Phi Gate, University of Arkansas

Fayetteville, Arkansas, 2012

Project Team:
Development Consultants, Inc., *landscape architect and civil engineer;* James H. Cone, *builder*

In 2008, alumnæ of Pi Beta Phi approached the University of Arkansas with the idea of giving a significant gift that would both enhance the campus and commemorate the 100th anniversary of the sorority's Arkansas chapter. Facilities Management Planning Group, which directs physical planning at the university, presented designs for gates of various sizes and degrees of elaboration at several key locations. The alumnæ committee chose the most prominent location nearest the heart of campus and in view of the university's iconic original building, Old Main. The plan also included the extension of an existing brick walk to the campus edge and a complete

redesign of two acres of landscape surrounding the site, including the re-establishment of an elm *alleé,* significant re-grading, and new utility infrastructure.

Todd Furgason's design for the gate was meant to connect with the long tradition of classical and gothic gates at American universities which, in turn, refer to numerous examples found at Oxford and Cambridge Universities. The University of Arkansas's own Collegiate Gothic master plan of 1925 had envisioned an Oxbridge Gothic campus of cloisters and quadrangles, battlements, and towers. The ten or so buildings built under this original plan established the basic urban framework for the Arkansas campus, and for a time elevated the expectation of architectural quality at the university. The Planning Group has tried to re-establish the urban design principles of the 1925 plan, and, where appropriate, implement its architectural vision. The Pi Beta Phi Gate realizes the monumental campus entrance as first envisioned in that plan.

Authenticity of materials and construction were important to the success of the project. The two primary materials were stone, cut by Quarra Stone Company, and metal, produced by Leonard Metal Art Works. The stone structure reaches almost 30 feet high and is composed of solid blocks of Indiana limestone, Batesville limestone, and granite, which

were laid in an eighth-inch bed of lime mortar. True wrought iron was used for the stationary parts of the metalwork—the crest and the surrounds—while the gate leaves were made of mild steel due to concerns about structural strength and operation. The design was detailed and constructed to create an enduring monument.

As a new campus entrance and commemorative gift, the gate is meant to evoke the traditions of higher education and the dignity of the academic mission of the university. This is perhaps best stated by the Latin inscription on the dedication plaque, which reads in translation:

"Enter to grow in wisdom; depart to serve with understanding and humility in good conscience. These gates stand in commemoration of one hundred years of Pi Beta Phi at the University of Arkansas. As an enduring testament to the generosity of their donor and monument to the immutable ideals of wisdom and truth in the shadows of which many esteemed have passed, pass, and will pass here in the laudable pursuit of knowledge, these gates were erected A.D. 2012."

Figure 1 (above): Pi Beta Phi Gate, University of Arkansas, Fayetteville, Arkansas. Overall view. Photograph by Todd Fugason.

Figure 2 (left): Detail of urn. Photograph by Todd Furgason.

Robert A. M. Stern Architects

New York, New York

FITNESS AND AQUATICS CENTER, BROWN UNIVERSITY
Providence, Rhode Island, 2012

PROJECT TEAM:
Robert A. M. Stern, *principal*; Gary Brewer, *project partner*; Chris Dickson, *project manager*; Eric Silinsh, *project assistant*; Matt Blumenthal, Scott Hirshson, Miyun Kang, Justin Latham, Julie Nymann, Tad Roemer, Yoko Suzuki, Roland Flores, Tin Lo, Tyler Virgil, and William Work

The Fitness and Aquatics Center provides much-needed athletic facilities and defines a new quadrangle at the gateway to Brown's evolving Erickson Athletic Complex. The new building brings the architectural character of the campus's historic brick buildings to the northeastern edge of the campus while also acknowledging Providence's tradition of robustly classical industrial buildings.

The Center is composed of three distinctly articulated parts: The head house, facing Hope Street, scaled to relate to the surrounding residential neighborhood, houses the exercise rooms, locker rooms, and the Nelson Fitness Center, a 10,000-square-foot multipurpose fitness loft. The David J. Zucconi '55 Varsity Strength and Conditioning Center faces the playing fields to the east. Bracketed between these two wings is the Katherine Moran Coleman Aquatics Center, with a 56-meter swimming pool, equipped for one- and three-meter diving, set one level below grade to reduce the mass of the building. The roof of the Aquatics Center features an array of solar panels, the largest hybrid solar-powered electrical and heating installation in the United States, generating enough power to light the building and enough thermal energy to heat the center's million-gallon pool.

The 50-foot Georgian Revival cupola and clock tower atop the new building was salvaged from Brown's Frederick Marvel Gymnasium (Clarke & Howe, 1927), which was demolished in 2002.

The landscaped Ittleson Quadrangle replaces the parking lot between the new building and the banal but functional 1970s Meehan Ice Rink and Pizzitola Gymnasium; a future new parking garage will be sensitively sited to the rear of the athletic complex.

Figure 1 (left): Fitness and Aquatics Center, Brown University. Detail of restored Marvel Cupola. Photograph by Peter Aaron/Otto for Robert A. M. Stern Architects.

Figure 2 (right): Fitness and Aquatics Center, Brown University. Exterior view from Hope Street. Photograph courtesy of Brown University.

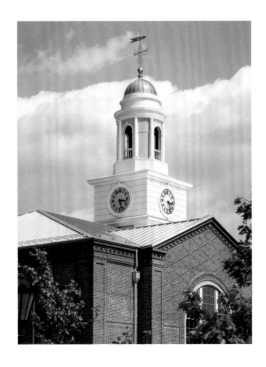

Appleton & Associates, Inc.

Santa Barbara, California

VILLA RAVELLO
Santa Barbara, California, 2011

PROJECT TEAM:
Marc Appleton, *Principal*
Domiane Forte and Ken Mineau, *Project Managers*
David Duarte, Alyssa Miller, Patrick Rauber,
Brian Speyerer

In the tradition of early nineteenth-century Mediterranean-inspired villas and pavilions like Schinkel and Perseus's Court Gardener's House at Park Sans-souci in Potsdam, Germany, Villa Ravello is a romantic country house far from Italy geographically, but nevertheless close to it in spirit. Santa Barbara's climate is a better match to the Mediterranean's than Germany, however, and this Villa also enjoys a panoramic view of the ocean over the tops of surrounding oak trees. It is home to the Owner's extensive collection of contemporary photographs and art, and the dining room canopy owes a small debt to the breakfast room of Sir John Soane's house in London.

Figure 1 (top): Villa Ravello, Santa Barbara, California. View of entrance. Photograph by Matt Walla.

Figure 2 (bottom): Villa Ravello, Santa Barbara, California, View of house from the rear. Photograph by Matt Walla.

Duncan G. Stroik Architect, LLC

South Bend, Indiana

A NEW ORGAN CASE FOR THE CATHEDRAL OF SAINT PAUL
Saint Paul, Minnesota, 2013

PROJECT TEAM:
Duncan G. Stroik and Forest E. Walton,
Ian Agrell, Agrell Architectural Carving, Ltd.,
decorative woodcarving

The Cathedral of Saint Paul in Minnesota is the *magnum opus* of French emigré architect Emmanuel Louis Masqueray and has one of the largest seating capacities of any Catholic cathedral in the United States. However, Masqueray's sketch for a cathedral organ circa 1905 was never realized. By 2010, the cathedral's Æolian-Skinner organ was in dire need of a major restoration and expansion. Stroik was commissioned to design a new organ case that would reflect the sophisticated classical architecture of the cathedral and accommodate a substantially enlarged instrument.

Masqueray's design for the organ case, documented in original sketches, would have risen in front of the cathedral's 26-foot diameter rose window, blocking it from view as in many French cathedrals. At the client's request, Stroik was able to preserve the visibility of the rose window while creating an organ screen in harmony with the surrounding Beaux-Arts interior, adapting motifs and details gleaned from Masqueray's drawings and the cathedral as built. The design was constrained by the size of the renovated organ along with the requirement to accommodate forty-eight choir members and musicians in the existing choir loft.

Twin circular towers house the largest of the organ pipes on either side of the rose window. The towers are supported by gilded pinecone corbels and culminate in bell-like domes supported by swags and crests. Angels holding a trumpet and a lyre surmount the Corinthian cornice at the point where the casework begins its curvilinear descent around the rose window; below, the cornice intersects a smaller central tower supporting the figure of St. Cecilia, patroness of music. Master British woodcarver Ian Agrell fabricated and installed the organ case in walnut, including its intricate hand-carved details. Intended to appear as if original to the building, the installation of the organ case took six days, after which parishioners entering the cathedral at Easter discovered this magnificent new organ case and heard the marvelous instrument within it.

Figure 1 (top left): New Organ Case for Cathedral of Saint Paul, Saint Paul, Minnesota. Overall view. Photograph by Liam Flahive.

Figure 2 (top right): New Organ Case for Cathedral of Saint Paul, Saint Paul, Minnesota. Detail of organ case. Photograph by Tim Schindler.

David Mayernik

South Bend, Indiana

Stage Sets for the Haymarket Opera Company of Chicago
2012—2013

Project Team:
Craig Trompeter, *Music Director*
Ellen Hargis, *Stage Director in Residence*
David Mayernik, *Set Designer*
Meriem Bahri, *Costume Designer*
Eric Peterson, *Lighting Designer*
Russell Wagner, *Logistics*

The design of opera sets was a natural corollary to the work of painters and architects in the seventeenth and eighteenth centuries. However, the modern renaissance of Baroque opera performance has not always been accompanied by sets of a sympathetic character. At the same time, many of the initiatives of the Early Music movement have affinities with the contemporary rebirth of classical art and architecture, though these two worlds have not fully connected. In fact, the design of sets for Baroque opera is a largely untapped vehicle for the modern classical movement, since it offers a paradigmatic opportunity for the integration of the arts.

The Haymarket Opera Company of Chicago commissioned David Mayernik to design sets for their February 2012 production of Marc-Antoine Charpentier's *La Descente d'Orphêe aux Enfers*, a seventeenth-century opera in two acts whose action is split between a pastoral setting and the underworld, and for the February 2013 performances of Henry Purcell's *Dido & Aeneas*, for which Mayernik designed palace and port scenes. The performances and staging received glowing reviews in the *New York Times*, the *Chicago Tribune*, *Chicago Sun-Times*, and the *Chicago Classical Review*, among others.

The idea of the sets was to convey not only the setting of each act—both the particular place and the mood—but also something of the narrative. Like music, the sets transmit tone and also help to carry the words along. They can in fact be "read" as supplementary stories, visually articulating what Charpentier's eloquent music and the words are saying. Seventeenth-century artists recognized the power of images to convey specific messages: character could be read in the gestures of a hand and the expressions of a face. But since imagery was also static, it had to convey multiple moments in the story—hinting at what came before and what was to come after. Each set, while distinct in character, also links to the others, bridging the disparate worlds of the drama's two acts—not unlike Charpentier's articulate music.

An ancient technique was employed for the side sets, the rotating prismatic *periaktoi* that Vitruvius described in his treatise. Conceived thousands of years ago, they are

still practical mechanisms for changing up to three scenes quickly (their modern iterations being those constantly changing billboards composed of rotating displays) and they allow variety in orientation and combinations. The changes of these sets are choreographed into the performances.

One of the primary means of what the Italians called *"l'inganno dell'occhio,"* deceiving the eye, was perspective. The illusion of space created on a two-dimensional surface demanded an ideal fixed viewpoint from which the illusion worked best; in court theaters it was the prince or king who occupied that seat. The Haymarket sets strive to provide not just one ideal spot, but the possibility of "deceptive" views throughout the theater; the perspective of the palace set integrates the orthogonal backcloth with the oblique *periaktoi*. Combining architectural and painterly illusionism, Baroque opera sets today offer the same challenges and opportunities they did in the era of Charpentier and Purcell.

Figure 1 (opposite): Set design for the Haymarket Opera production of Purcell's *Dido and Aeneas.* Palace scene. Painting by David Mayernik.

Figure 2 (above): Set design for the Haymarket Opera production of Charpentier's *La Descente d'Orphèe aux Enfers.* Underworld scene. Painting by David Mayernik.

Figure 3 (left): Haymarket Opera production of Charpentier's *La Descente d'Orphèe aux Enfers.* Performance with Peter van de Graaff as Apollo. Photograph by Charles Osgood Photography.

Ex Libris

Albert Speer: Architecture 1932-1942

By Léon Krier
New York: Monacelli Press, 2012.

Reviewed by Steven W. Semes

IMAGINE A COURTROOM DRAMA: Classical architecture stands accused of complicity in Nazi crimes against humanity. The clamorous prosecution team declares that the formal language derived from ancient Greece and Rome is irrevocably tainted by its associations with Hitler (and, to a lesser extent, Mussolini) and so, like the swastika and the fasces, must be eliminated from modern visual culture. The lone defense counsel counters that classical architecture has no fixed political significance and that the truly criminal collaboration is that of modernist architecture with the global industrial corporate state, of which the Nazi system was a pioneer. Both prosecution and defense focus on Exhibit A, the work of Albert Speer, architect of the most audacious projects commissioned by the National Socialist state and designed in close collaboration with the Führer. Prosecutors point to Speer's classicizing work as evidence of the accused's guilt; defense counsel asks the jury to look closely at Speer's architecture, suggesting that such "elegant" and "sublime" designs should be accepted for their aesthetic merit despite their reprehensible political use. But the jury asks, "Is Speer's work really classical?" While it makes obvious use of classical motifs, it is also reveals similarities to modernist proposals of the same era. The complicity of Speer with the regime is clearly evident, but, as the judge reminds the jury, Speer is not on trial, classical architecture is. If Speer is not an appropriate representative of the tradition, then the tradition itself cannot be condemned based on his work alone. Finding the prosecution's case unpersuasive, the jury acquits classical architecture on all counts, while privately admitting concern at the weakness of the defense's case.

But this is fiction: the real trial ended with the condemnation of classical architecture and a campaign to destroy the reputation of the defense counsel for having dared to defend it. With the re-publication of *Albert Speer: Architecture 1932-1942*, originally published in 1985 following a 1978 article, that lone defender, Léon Krier, offers us Exhibit A in an elegantly-designed package full of imagery both seductive and disturbing. The book argues passionately against the prosecution's attempt to link classical architecture with repellent political values and it amply documents the designs of Speer, but neither Krier nor his critics have addressed the question that most concerned our fictitious jury: Is Speer an appropriate representative of the classical tradition in architecture and can his work be cited either to condemn or to defend it? In my view, both prosecution and defense have fundamentally erred by ignoring this question.

The moral and legal judgment on Albert Speer for his role as Hitler's Armaments Minister was irrevocably handed down at Nuremberg and ratified by his subsequent imprisonment. The aesthetic judgment of the architectural establishment was no less severe and was extended beyond Speer himself to embrace the entire classical tradition;

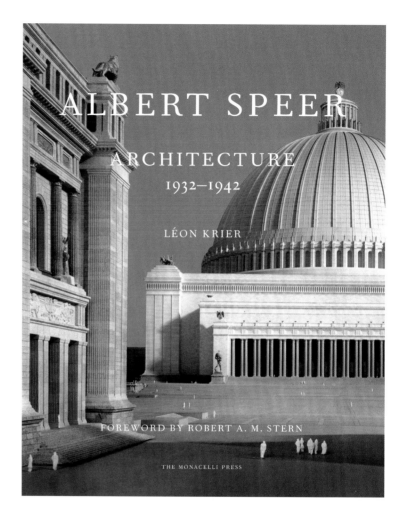

this was condemned as the official style of totalitarianism, while modernism was praised as the built expression of democracy and progress. Post-war critics attacked traditionalist pre-war architects for bending their aesthetic values to serve the propaganda aims of politically and morally repellent regimes; but in a curious reversal, the critics allowed their political and moral judgments to be swayed by their pro-modernist aesthetic commitments. In order to uphold the innocence of the modern, the classical had to be found guilty, even in the face of contrary evidence. We now know that the relation between style and politics during the inter-war period was much more complex and that both classical and modernist architectures were used at different times and for different reasons by both autocratic and democratic regimes. The political content of specific architectural forms, as Krier correctly asserts, is precisely zero; the suppression of classical architecture is simply aesthetic prejudice masquerading as political-moral judgment. But Krier goes further, arguing that the real "criminal" element in the story was industrial production and mass-culture, both of which became core values for modernist architecture and have led to devastating effects on the built and natural environments, as well as on social and cultural life. This, in Krier's view, prompts a reconsideration of the classical alternative and Speer's contribution to it.

The book amply illustrates Speer's architectural and urban design work—virtually unavailable elsewhere—principally the massive projects for the center of Berlin, many of which were executed, only to be demolished following the defeat of the regime. Although these projects vary considerably in quality and interest, a dispassionate aesthetic judgment on the North-South Axis, the Fürher's Palace, the New Chancellery, the unbuilt Great Hall, and a number of other massive projects remains difficult, despite Krier's expressed admiration. The great disappointment of this book is that it offers us the imagery and the political argument, but not the kind of formal analysis that would allow us to make a separate aesthetic judgment. Lars Olof Larsson's essay helpfully puts Speer's work into its historical and cultural context, but does not thoroughly analyze any of his buildings. Krier apparently assumes Speer's standing as a classical architect, confident that his rehabilitation will exonerate the tradition as a whole. But to judge the work's quality as classical architecture, we must look beyond the emblematic use of classical devices to grasp its formal conception and language; most importantly, we must judge its character and effects. Based on the documentation presented in the book and viewing it in the context of the historical panorama of classical architecture, Speer appears an inappropriate champion for a tradition far more convincingly represented by many of his contemporaries, and the character of his work—not just its style or symbolism—reveals close and inescapable affinities with the social and political aims of his client.

What makes a design classical? The question cannot be answered in this brief review, but it also cannot be reduced to the presence of columns, arches, domes, figural sculpture, or a reliance on bilateral symmetry and an urban scheme of streets and squares. It is not only these externals that make a work classical, but an inner compositional ordering system that coordinates and justifies all of these, uniting them and subordinating them to humanizing intentions. Speer's projects may present these externals, but they are conspicuously lacking in the compositional order of classicism; the buildings relentlessly repeat identical units and underscore the industrial mass-produced character of the designs.

If we compare his projects with earlier classical monuments in Berlin, such as the Brandenburg Gate or the old Reichstag (also illustrated in the book), we notice that Speer's elevations are relentlessly horizontal, their repetitive march of identical windows continuing indefinitely, in contrast to the proportionally felicitous subdivisions of the older buildings. The Führer's Palace, for example, has two tiers of columns aligned across its façade (which extends for 240 meters or 780 feet), but the columns are in a contrasting material and the superimposed orders are not in vertical registration. This has the effect of dividing the elevation into two horizontal stripes, in contrast with the scheme of vertically-proportioned bays characteristic of classical buildings. Krier says this elevation is the same width as Vanvitelli's Regia at Caserta, but what a difference in compositional strategy! Missing in almost all of Speer's work is a sense of Vitruvian eurhythmy—the healthy dose of variety and movement that would relieve its crushing monotony.

Also lacking is what architectural theorist and mathematician Nikos Salingaros calls "scaling coherence," the breakdown of an architectural composition into a series of judiciously graduated scale levels, from the whole to its smallest details. Classical architecture, with its recursive, fractal composition of parts and wholes, naturally produces scaling coherence, so that as the building increases in size, the number of scale levels increases too. What impresses us about very large classical buildings—the Paris Opera or the United States Capitol, for example—is not their size, but their *enrichment.* As one approaches, the building does not simply get bigger, it reveals new levels of detail. In many modernist buildings, the number of scale levels is minimal, perhaps only two—the whole and the repeated modular unit; but instead of expressing largeness, as Geoffrey Scott observed, such a structure expresses only smallness magnified. Speer himself, in a brief "Foreward" to Krier's book, recognized that "there is no way to fight the absence of scale." The use of ornament integrated into the composition at various scale levels would have helped, but here sculptural groups are introduced as independent units, unintegrated with the composition of the whole. The lack of scaling coherence in Speer's buildings and exterior spaces produces an effect not of exaltation or celebration but of alienation and ennui, and it is exactly here, in the evocation of architectural character at large scale, that the aesthetic and the political intentions of the designer and client clearly converge, as Speer himself candidly admitted.

Much attention has been devoted to the apparent gigantism of Speer's projects. The Forum of Trajan in Rome—built to celebrate the Emperor who actually accomplished the world domination that Hitler dreamed of—was less than one-quarter the size of the lower level of the Great Square in front of the Great Hall of Berlin. Ancient Roman monuments, however grand they appeared, respected the observer's perceptive powers and the human need for orientation and enclosure. The Italian critic Ugo Ojetti, writing against the similarly megalomaniac (but more interesting) scheme for the historic center of Rome by Speer's contemporary Armando Brasini, said that the architect had confused grandeur with vastness: "Vast, indeed, was the Roman Empire, but not all the streets and squares of ancient Rome." The obsession with buildings and spaces of excessive dimensions is a modernist preoccupation rather than a classical one, intended to accommodate the immense crowds assembled by the social vision of Speer's client.

The aesthetic impulse behind this gigantism was undoubtedly Speer's adoption—at Hitler's insistence—of the sublime as an artistic ideal. Romantic artists and poets embraced the sublime as an awed response to prodigious natural phenomena, and architects sometimes sought sublime effects in buildings or spaces having analogous properties, as in the proposals of the French "revolutionary" architect Boullée. Krier notes the wall of skyscrapers overlooking New York's Central Park as another example of the urban sublime. Many of us may admire such effects, but they are rare in an artistic tradition that values attunement to the human endowment and commitment to life lived in civilized community rather than in the wilderness or an anonymous mass-culture. The Romantic sublime sought a response of awed submission before the powers of Nature; Hitler's sublime demands our awed submission before the powers of the State, again indicating the convergence of aesthetic and political aims. But, as Geoffrey Scott made clear, the sublime as an aesthetic ideal is *anti-classical,* however seductive it may be in specific instances.

In stylistic terms, Speer's designs participate in the "stripped classicism" that sought to reconcile the classical and the modern, and which, in the 1930s, was the leading fashion in most advanced countries. In the hands of the Italian Marcello Piacentini, the Frenchman Auguste Perret, the Briton Charles Holden, the Swede Gunnar Asplund, or the American Paul Cret, the style could achieve a certain rationalism and elegance, if not the desired reconciliation of two antithetical conceptions of architecture. In Speer's hands it became a brutal compromise, a worst-of-both-worlds scenario in which all that was beautiful, graceful, and humane in classicism was eliminated, along with whatever was dynamic and idealistic in modernism. But the uniqueness of Speer's work lay not in its style, but in its manipulation of character. He himself wrote that his buildings strove "to achieve (political) effects through architectural means…(the viewer) is right to detect Hitler's desire for power and the submission of others in my buildings. The main character of my architecture expressed this urge." That modernist critics—and to an extent Krier also—do not distinguish between style and character leads to the error of rejecting the first for the misuse of the second. The classical was not fundamental to Speer's work, but a dominating, intimidating character was; and this might just as well have been achieved by a modernist style as by a classical one.

So on what basis can Speer's work be used either to attack or to defend the classical tradition? Lacking in classical composition, without scaling coherence, and envisioning the city as a set of vast open spaces constituting an immense stage for rituals of dehumanizing submission to the state, Speer's vision for Berlin could not be farther from the humanism of the classical city represented by Rome, Nancy, Edinburgh, Washington, or pre-Hitler Berlin, or as imagined by Leon Battista Alberti, Camillo Sitte, Gustavo Giovannoni, or Henry Hope Reed. This is not the work of an architect who respectfully places himself in the stream of tradition, but of one who cynically manipulates imagery drawn from the tradition in order to subvert the human values historically embodied by it. In my view, Speer betrayed the artistic tradition of Western classicism in architecture as thoroughly as he betrayed the values of Western humanism in the political-moral sphere.

We can only commend Léon Krier for the courage with which he offers his spirited defense of the classical, but he has chosen the wrong hero in this struggle. Albert Speer is not an appropriate model for a continuing classical tradition in the modern world and attempting his rehabilitation does not advance the classical cause. We must look instead to such contemporaries as Edwin Lutyens, John Russell Pope, Bernard Maybeck, Arthur Brown, Jr., and growing numbers of practitioners around the world today—Léon Krier himself is an example— whose work points to a viable contemporary classicism and a commitment to building cities that are beautiful, sustainable, and just.

LEON KRIER RESPONDS:

Hitler's and Speer's buildings, avenues, and landscapes are not the world either of us want to live in; yet if they had been built and the Nazi system buried, they would have become an architectural and aesthetic experience of breathtaking (literally) quality for free and undamaged individuals. To deny that possibility is, in my opinion, an intellectual mistake. Such denial reminds me of Gabriel Axel's film "Babette's Feast," when Protestant old men discuss whether they should accept Babette's invitation to a sumptuous dinner. "But what if we like it?" one of them anxiously interjects, to which the town elder responds, "We won't talk about it." The main thing is to give these issues a public airing and then, one day, everyone will be able to give their feelings a true rather than a lying voice. Again, that is my opinion and hope. Our worst enemies can be great artists. That is the way of the world.

Steven W. Semes is the Editor of The Classicist *and Associate Professor in the University of Notre Dame School of Architecture.*

An Infinity of Graces: Cecil Ross Pinsent, an English Architect in the Italian Landscape

By Ethne Clarke
W.W. Norton & Company, New York-London, 2013.

Reviewed by Judith Spencer Chatfield

CECIL ROSS PINSENT is at last the subject of long-deserved, in-depth attention in the realm of architecture and garden design in the first half of the twentieth century. His Italianate gardens are sensitive interpretations of classic Italian models on an intimate scale, consisting of closely interwoven garden rooms well-related to their houses and surrounding landscapes. *An Infinity of Graces,* a biography by Ethne Clarke, finally tackles this subject.

An Englishman, Pinsent was born in Montevideo, Uruguay in 1884. He trained in London as an architect at the Architectural Association and Royal Academy School of Architecture, where he was tutored by Sir Reginald Blomfield, author of *The Formal Garden in England.* Subsequently, he was employed in the firms of E. T. Hall, E. W. Montford, and C. E. Mallows, the latter being an exponent of formal garden design. The recipient of a travel grant, Pinsent made a fateful ten-month journey to Italy in 1908-1909, during which his encounter with Bernard and Mary Berenson was to launch him on a notable career catering primarily to expatriates in Tuscany.

At the urging of Mary Berenson he teamed up with Geoffrey Scott, her protégée. This proved to be an uneven partnership, Pinsent being the more productive partner. Scott had vision and taste, but was lacking in self-motivation and practicality. During this period, Pinsent and Scott renovated the farmhouse purchased by Berenson at Settignano, creating a comfortable home and library, while transforming the property into a terraced formal garden. Pinsent and Scott ended their business partnership after World War I, but remained friends.

Pinsent was inspired by classical Italian gardens, especially Villa Gamberaia for its transitional spaces, but designed gardens for contemporary use, such as the garden room at Villa Capponi with its swimming pool. He cleverly incorporated framed views of the countryside beyond the gardens. Pinsent's most successful creation is the ingeniously-sited Villa le Balze, at Fiesole. Perched on a narrow strip of hillside, he designed the interlocking house and garden rooms for American scholar Charles Augustus Strong. Work on the house and garden continued over a number of years with interruptions, starting in 1912 and concluding in 1922.

Clarke includes in an appendix "Giardini moderni all'italiana," an essay in which Pinsent sets forth his principles of garden design. This is invaluable for appreciation of his work, especially the careful architectural considerations in his construction of garden rooms not only to be satisfying within but also when viewed as a whole from above. Flowers are permitted to enhance the design, but not to compete with its clarity. He writes, "The first characteristic of a garden in the Italian style is orderly symmetry. The modern stylized garden should have order and dignity in the area nearest to the house, so that the view from the window provides a calm and restful experience…. At the boundaries of the garden we place woodlands and other more practical, less stylized (i.e., natural) elements." Regarding general design, "The individual areas of the modern private garden should be small rather than large and so more in harmony with modern life, which is more intimate than in the past…..The modern garden is like the house laid open to the air, with rooms that when passed through provide a variety of impressions rather than having everything revealed at once." He continues in this vein to list the preferred choice of plant material, ideally suggesting permanence of structure throughout the seasons. He is specific about which flowers and vines are suitable. His taste was at variance with Edith Wharton's, who eschewed flowers in an Italian garden, and criticized him for including deciduous trees and lawns, which were not traditional in these gardens.

Much of Clarke's book revolves around the expatriate community of Florence in the early twentieth century, the city's attraction having been fueled by contemporary writers and the personalities who settled there. Her fascination with the Anglo-Americans who lived abroad reflects her own expatriate life as an American living in England. She was informed by the Italian garden books of Georgina Masson and

Edith Wharton, which triggered her love affair with Italian gardens beginning in 1986. Harold Acton set her on her quest to research Cecil Pinsent saying, "You know, you really ought to find out everything you can about Pinsent. So little about him is known with any accuracy." Clarke had access to personal letters belonging to Pinsent's relatives, as well as memories and photographs of Iris Origo's villa La Foce thanks to Origo's daughter, Benedetta. In addition, his family turned over six photograph albums compiled by Pinsent. These provide personal glimpses of the man Pinsent was, who otherwise remains an enigma; they whet my appetite for more information.

I wish the book had included more plans of his garden layouts. The small dimensions of many of the photographs make them almost illegible, which is frustrating, and these old reproduced black and white photographs could have been manipulated digitally for greater contrast. I suspect it was not economically feasible to include color photographs in the book, but doing so would have enhanced it greatly. The back cover displays a view of Villa Gamberaia, which strongly influenced Pinsent, but is not his design and is, therefore, misleading. The bibliography should have included important works written about the classic Italian gardens that held sway during the period in which Pinsent was working. Titles by Charles A. Platt, Charles Latham, G. S. Elgood, Marie Luise Gothein, Geoffrey Jellicoe with C. J. Shepherd, Rose Standish Nichols, and Luigi Dami, as well as the catalogue of the 1931 garden show held in Florence are unfortunate omissions in my view.

Pinsent has long fascinated me, and his few well-preserved gardens are enchanting and serene, as well as being livable. The week before I was asked to write this review, I was at the Villa Spada in Rome, now the Irish Embassy. I hadn't realized that Pinsent had worked on the property and Clarke does not discuss this garden. I asked for details and the Ambassador gave me a copy of *Villa Spada* (Istituto Poligrafico e Zecca dello Stato, Rome, 2007), a book not included in Clarke's bibliography. When I stepped down into the pocket-sized lateral southern garden room, it felt familiar. It consists of two rows of trimmed orange trees, with a small fountain basin set in a lush lawn. It is hemmed in by a surrounding wall, has neat gravel paths, offers a feeling of repose, and is snugly sited next to the rooms of the *villino,*

which open on to it: All of this spoke of Pinsent's *oeuvre.* I would concur with the author of *Villa Spada,* Carla Benocci, that it is likely Pinsent had a hand in its updating.

It is known that a permit was filed in 1927 with Roman authorities naming Cecil Pinsent as project designer and Stefano Gentiloni Severi as engineer for improvement work within the *villino.* The pre-existing garden was said to have been in good condition when Countess Nora Khuen purchased the villa the year before. The *contessa* was an Anglo-Florentine conversant with Pinsent's garden designs, and it is highly probable that she wished him to edit the garden. Aerial photographs taken shortly before that date show the garden masked by dense foliage, which Pinsent would not have tolerated. Furthermore, detailed descriptions of the gardens at Villa Spada in 1889 specify small round fountain basins in the north and south gardens. Today's garden has a small scalloped basin in the same location to the south, a smaller-scale version of the large one in the entrance court. This is identical to the graceful fountain Pinsent designed for Iris Origo's study garden at La Foce the very same year, 1927, when he worked at Villa Spada. A rear portion of the small lateral garden was lost when a swimming pool was installed, but enough remains to convince me of Cecil Pinsent's intervention.

Clarke has been researching Cecil Pinsent for over fifteen years and writes with sympathy for her subject. I hope material about him is not exhausted, and that eventually a fuller work will emerge. Clarke has included Pinsent's detailed chronology of his work, which is a useful jumping-off point for future investigations.

Judith Spencer Chatfield is a garden historian in Sharon, Connecticut. She is the author of A Tour of Italian Gardens, The Classic Italian Garden, Gardens of the Italian Lakes, *and* The Boboli Gardens *(with Francesco Guerrieri).*

The Church Building as a Sacred Place: Beauty, Transcendence, and the Eternal

By Duncan G. Stroik
Chicago: Liturgy Training Publications, 2012.

Reviewed by John H. Cluver, AIA

"WHY IS IT THAT FEW OF OUR CHURCHES built in recent decades intimate that the church building itself and the celebrations taking place within it are sacred?" This is the fundamental question asked by Duncan Stroik in the opening paragraph of his insightful book, *The Church Building as a Sacred Space,* a collection of twenty-three essays written over a period of two decades exploring fundamental principles of Catholic church design, the state of religious architecture today, the role of modernism and modernity in ecclesiastical architecture, and what steps can and should be taken to renew the sense of the sacred in our churches. Although many of the chapters are reprints of previously-published articles, they combine nicely with a fresh introduction and three new essays to create a book that is a critical text (in both tone and importance) for anyone interested in the future of sacred architecture. The articles vary in length and character, but all are very readable (with the occasional Latin word or phrase added for emphasis) and are as one would expect from an author who has dedicated several decades to the study and design of Catholic churches. More than just a collection of essays, the book covers a wide range of topics conveniently organized as individual chapters with several key concepts woven throughout.

As implied by the title of the book, one of these key concepts is the sense of the sacred and how it is found (or not found) in church architecture. Stroik's introduction does an excellent job of setting the framework for this idea and the importance of the church building as the equivalent of "church documents in stone." Additional chapters delve more deeply into this theme, starting with the six definitions of a church building: liturgical, sacramental, a home for liturgical elements, devotional, iconographic/symbolic, and sacred. They continue with the recognition that the church is not just a worship space for a congregation but also a House of God worthy of being beautiful, durable, and symbolic. This point is supported by a careful review of the principles of church design and the relationships between such elements as the altar, sanctuary, tabernacle, nave, ambo, and façade, which serves as a great primer for architects, congregations, students, and indeed anyone interested in the creation of a proper church.

Another recurring theme is the role of classicism in church design and, in contrast, the failure of modernism to create ecclesiastical architecture that expresses the sense of the sacred. Stroik is particularly adept in analyzing the historical transition from traditional to modernist approaches to church design and how that has led to architecture that does not distinguish between the sacred and the profane. This is illustrated by a critique of Richard Meier's "Church of the Year 2000" in Rome that reveals how that project reflects an architectural approach

uninterested in spirituality and a Church uncomfortable with its cultural heritage. This chapter contrasts nicely with a later one presenting Stroik's design for All Saints Church in Walton, Kentucky, which illustrates many of the points he raises elsewhere in the book and to prove, as a another pastor visiting the newly completed project remarked, "Well, I guess we are allowed to build traditional churches once again."

Additional essays provide commentary on the relationship between contemporary culture and sacred architecture. After excursions into such topics as the trend of the church as a performance space, the inversion of values (and spending levels) with respect to building churches and private houses, and the growing trend (driven by tourism) of churches as "galleries of sacred art," Stroik focuses on the recapturing the sense of the sacred and creating beautiful, durable, art-filled churches once again. The essay entitled "Can We Afford Not to Build Beautiful Churches?" is the highlight of the book, pulling together many of the ideas explored elsewhere to make the case for the church's critical civic and spiritual role, how that was lost in the past century, and how it can be enlivened anew. To that end, Stroik provides a helpful chapter with advice to pastors and congregations on how best

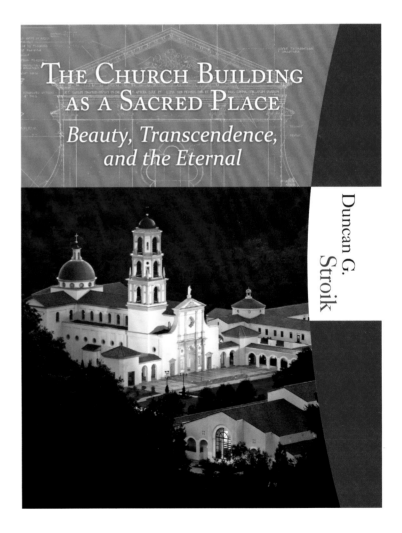

to create or renovate a church, focusing on practical concerns such as selecting an architect, balancing the project's program and budget, and building well.

The insights provided throughout the book are illustrated by numerous photographs, averaging roughly one per page. These are a combination of historical and contemporary examples of church design, the latter heavily focused on the author's own built works. Even as some images are full bleed pages, others are disappointingly small given the intricate beauty found in some of them. The book also provides information to help those wishing to delve further into the topic, including three appendices with a list of canonical documents pertaining to church architecture, an informative dimensional comparison of many of the great churches in the world, and a similar study of the six great baldacchinos in Rome. Other written resources, both historical and contemporary, are listed throughout the body of the book. In aggregate, *Church Building as a Sacred Place* is a vital resource for architects, pastors, and anyone interested in the future of church architecture.

John H. Cluver, AIA, LEED AP practices architecture and historic preservation in Philadelphia, PA as a partner in the firm Voith & Mactavish Architects, LLP.

Figure 1 (above): Chapel of Saint Thomas Aquinas University, Santa Paula, California, 2009, by Duncan Stroik Architect. From *The Church Building as a Sacred Space: Beauty, Transcendence, and the Eternal,* by Duncan Stoik, Chicago Liturgy Training Publications, 2012. Photograph by Schafphoto. Reproduced with permission.

Grand Central: Gateway to a Million Lives

By John Belle and Maxine Rhea Leighton
New York: W.W. Norton & Company, 2012

Grand Central: How a Train Station Transformed America

By Sam Roberts
New York: Grand Central Publishing, 2013

Grand Central Terminal: 100 Years of a New York Landmark

By Anthony W. Robins
New York: Abrams Books, 2013

Reviewed by Francis Morrone

"NEW YORK," WROTE HENRY HOPE REED in 1967, "is one of the great classical cities of the world"—like Rome, St. Petersburg, Paris, Washington, Vienna, and Dublin. "To the vast sweep of the classical heritage New York has even made its own special contribution in the form of the classical bank, the classical railroad station, the classical lamp post, the classical avenue in a new dimension, and the classical department store."

Our surviving classical railroad station, Grand Central Terminal, is what we call a New York City "icon." By that overused word we mean that Grand Central is among the handful of images—others include the Statue of Liberty, the Brooklyn Bridge, and the Empire State Building—that immediately conjure "New York" in the viewer's mind. It can be used for an "establishing shot" in a movie or TV show. At Grand Central, this is equally true of both the building's exterior and its interior—it may indeed be unique among New York icons in that respect. An iconic structure earns its status by being a striking, distinctive object, but it goes well beyond just that to embody meanings that give a place its sense of itself, and of its self-worth.

What, exactly, makes Grand Central Terminal iconic? It was never the busiest railroad station in Manhattan, let alone America or the world. Though grand, it never possessed the awe-inspiring grandeur of Pennsylvania Station (demolished fifty years ago) across town. For starters, Grand Central is a building that has accrued stories, amounting to a mythology that has been embroidered and retold for nearly as long as the structure has stood, which, as it happens, is one hundred years. Among these stories are the myths and legends it embodies—Franklin Delano Roosevelt and his private siding, "mole people" in disused tunnels, or the Twentieth Century Limited. Then there are the artistic associations, including Alfred Hitchcock's film *North by Northwest* and Mark Helprin's novel *Winter's Tale.* All of this is fun and all of it

resonates with New Yorkers. But at the deepest level, Grand Central possesses its lofty status because its architecture inspires and ennobles us. When we say that an iconic structure embodies a place's sense of its own self-worth, we may pause to consider that the classical forms of Grand Central, handled with supreme confidence in the service of what was at the time the most advanced technology, suggest to New Yorkers that their city, while in so many ways unique, also stands in a proud succession—the inheritor and interpreter of a proud tradition of classical architecture and classical values.

Many books have been written about the terminal, and David Marshall's *Grand Central*, published in 1946, remains a favorite of mine, both for its effortless readability and its wealth of detail not found in other books. It's breezy, journalistic, anecdotal, yet deeply informative. Alas, it's also a trove of period obtuseness (its writer really, really hates Jules-Félix Coutan's sculptural group on 42nd Street) and casual xenophobia. Carl W. Condit, the great historian of the Chicago skyscraper, turned his attention to New York in 1980 with a magisterial two-volume work called *The Port of New York.* This minutely (and sometimes confusingly) detailed history of the city's "rail and terminal system" devotes much of volume two to the design, construction, and operation of our now one-hundred-year-old Grand Central Terminal. *The Port of New York*, sadly out of print, is as yet unsurpassed as a description of the improbably complicated, Rube Goldberg-esque rail and waterfront terminal operations that once were (and are no longer) the economic lifeblood of New York, and the parts on Grand Central do not disappoint. In 2006, Peter Pennoyer and Anne Walker gave us *The Architecture of Warren & Wetmore*, a much-needed monograph on Grand Central's design architects. Now three important new books on Grand Central have been published in celebration of its centennial year.

Figure 1 (above): Sculptural group by Jules-Félix Coutan atop main façade, from *Grand Central Terminal: 100 Years of a New York Landmark* by the New York Transit Museum and Anthony W. Robins, Stewart, Tabori & Chang, 2012. Photograph by Frank English. Reproduced with permission.

First a little history: Grand Central Terminal came into being between 1903 and 1913, when an earlier facility on the same site straddling Park Avenue north of 42nd Street, built to handle the operations of steam-powered trains, was replaced by a new terminal to serve the electric trains that put an end to the noisome and smoky conditions of the old yards. Since tracks and yards could now be safely placed underground, Grand Central was converted by its owners—the New York Central and New York, New Haven & Hartford Railroads—into an underground facility, with two levels of subterranean tracks (a first for any railroad station), and vast subsurface marshaling yards. This allowed the railroad to build upon its "air rights" (a term said to have been coined by the New York Central Railroad's chief engineer, William J. Wilgus), stretching roughly from Lexington to Madison Avenues and from 42nd to 50th Streets. "From the air would be taken wealth," John Belle and Maxine Rhea Leighton quote Wilgus as saying in their *Grand Central: Gateway to a Million Lives* and one of the three important new books on Grand Central. Thus was born "Terminal City," the collection of mostly high-rise buildings—for hotels, offices, apartments, and private clubs—that would surround the terminal head house, define a newly elegant Park Avenue, and form the nucleus of Midtown Manhattan, which beginning in the 1910s and 1920s displaced lower Manhattan as the city's central business district.

John Belle is a principal in the Manhattan architectural firm of Beyer Blinder Belle, best known for its restoration and renovation work, Grand Central being their crowning accomplishment. The terminal had sadly deteriorated for decades when, in the 1990s, Metro-North, the commuter railroad serving points north of the city, undertook a monumental renovation that restored the building's architectural glory and gave it new life as a retail and dining destination.

As everyone knows, Manhattan's other legendary railroad station, Pennsylvania Station, was demolished after standing for only a little more than a half-century. After World War II, the great railroads—Penn Station's owners, the Pennsylvania Railroad, had actually once been the biggest business corporation in America—suffered such steep declines that their only alternative was to attempt to cash in on the urban real estate they owned. Unlike Penn Station, however, Grand Central survived to be designated under the 1965 law that gave New York City broad powers to order the preservation in perpetuity of historic buildings. In 1968, Penn Central Corporation (formed of the merger of the once arch-rival Pennsylvania and New York Central Railroads) proposed to erect a Marcel Breuer-designed tower atop the terminal head house. Mind you, the northern office annex of the head house complex had already been replaced by the hulking Pan American Airways (now MetLife) Building. The new tower would preserve the historic structure, but at the expense of imposing upon it a gigantic modernist skyscraper. The city's Landmarks Preservation Commission basically said to Penn Central "You've got to be kidding." But Penn Central was not kidding. The railroad claimed the landmark designation was an unconstitutional taking of property rights, and brought suit. New York City fought all the way to the Supreme Court, whose 1978 ruling upheld the constitutionality of the Landmarks Law, and Grand Central was saved. But was it?

Penn Central let the place run down. World War II blackout paint had never been removed from windows. Cigarette smoke had blackened the "Sky Ceiling" of the Main Concourse. Garish advertisements shouted from every wall—most infamously the immense Kodak Colorama slung across the east windows of the Main Concourse. Automobiles revolved on display stands on the Concourse floor. The nadir came in the 1980s when many homeless people made Grand Central their home.

When Metro-North took over Grand Central's operation, they took a cue from Washington, D.C., where Daniel H. Burnham's magnificent Union Station had been recently brought back from the dead. Much of the Union Station team was reassembled in New York and Grand Central underwent its miraculous transformation, becoming more visited and more iconic than ever before, even as its role as the rail gateway to New York disappeared with the cessation of long-distance service to and from the terminal. (Today Grand Central is strictly a suburban commuting facility.) Indeed, Grand Central became the very symbol of New York City's renaissance as a whole. A building doesn't get any more iconic than that.

Just about every architect, classicist or modernist, professes an admiration of Grand Central Terminal. It would be absurd not to admire the building for its compact, efficient planning, its system of ramps, and the functional ease so different not only from the current, dreadful Penn Station but also from the old, majestic Penn Station. Commentators on Grand Central rightly ascribe the superb planning to a firm of architects from Minnesota, Reed & Stem, and to New York Central's Wilgus. It's no less fashionable today than it's ever been to consider the terminal's second team of architects, New York's Warren & Wetmore, as interlopers, even despoilers, who claimed credit for elements of the design that were not theirs. It is thus that modernists have been able to claim Grand Central as their own. Rightly considered, they would say, the terminal is first and foremost outstanding for its engineering and planning, the handiwork of Reed & Stem; Warren & Wetmore came on board later (at the behest of Whitney Warren's cousin, William K. Vanderbilt, the head of the New York Central) to dress it up—and thankfully they did not go over the top in the dressing up.

Warren, clearly, was responsible for the crowning statuary group on Forty-Second Street opposite Park Avenue. Henry Hope Reed felt this to be "the best piece of monumental sculpture in America," as Belle and Leighton report. Yet so little regarded has it been in most of the years since it was installed (June 1914), that writers on Grand Central, including Condit, Kurt C. Schlichting, and even Belle and Leighton have rendered its sculptor's name as Jules-*Alexis* Coutan, not the correct Jules-Félix Coutan. Why is this mistake so telling? In the early twentieth century, Coutan was as famous a sculptor as France could boast. His works in public places in Paris are so numerous (e.g., *France de la Renaissance* on the glorious Pont Alexandre III) that he must be ranked among that classical city's principal embellishers. Yet his was among those sad academic careers that met the big broom of the modernist rebellion and got swept into the dustbin of history. The idea was that an artist like Coutan—professor at the École des Beaux-Arts, design director of Sèvres porcelain, creator of the Fontaine Coutan that set off the Eiffel Tower at the 1889 exposition, and an establishment figure *par excellence*—would never be remembered again.

Inside, the French painter Paul Helleu contributed the design, or the idea, for the Sky Ceiling—the mural painting in gold on a rich blue-green of the constellations in reverse. The original ceiling fresco was done by the Australian (and Beaux-Arts-trained) Charles Basing and his team, I presume with Helleu nowhere in the neighborhood. By the 1940s this original fresco had deteriorated and it was replaced by a panel mural (painted by Charles Gulbrandsen), which is what we see today. David Garrard Lowe, at the time of the renovation, in 1995, suggested that this mural be ditched. "With a vigorous revival of realistic painting now under way," Lowe wrote, "why not have one of the new realists devise an entirely new decorative scheme?"

Belle's and Leighton's *Grand Central*, unsurprisingly, provides the greatest wealth of detail on the profound renovation of the terminal, including a detailed section on the construction of the new east staircase in the Main Concourse. The book reproduces a 1911 drawing that clearly indicates that Whitney Warren intended matching stairs at the east and west ends of the concourse. Of course, when the terminal opened in 1913, only a west staircase had been built. Beyer Blinder Belle asked the Landmarks Preservation Commission for permission to add

Warren's "lost" staircase to the concourse. As the book shows, permission was granted, but with the proviso that the new staircase be both compatible with and significantly differentiated from the earlier staircase —to show that it is "of our time." To that end, the new staircase is of similar form and identical materials to the older one, but of simplified design, with smoothly finished rail terminations rather than the elaborately carved terminations of Warren's west staircase. This, in my view, was a mistake, the result of muddled modernist thinking about avoiding "faked historic material." That said, I've no doubt that were the job to be done today, the differentiation would be even starker—that perhaps, as Belle and Leighton say was suggested back at the time, the new stair would be of steel. (Indeed, if the Breuer tower were proposed today, I believe it just might be approved.) Another plus to Belle's and Leighton's book is its stunning contemporary photographs by Peter Aaron and James Rudnick. The book was originally published in 2000, to commemorate the completion (more or less) of the renovation, and has been revised and reissued for the centennial.

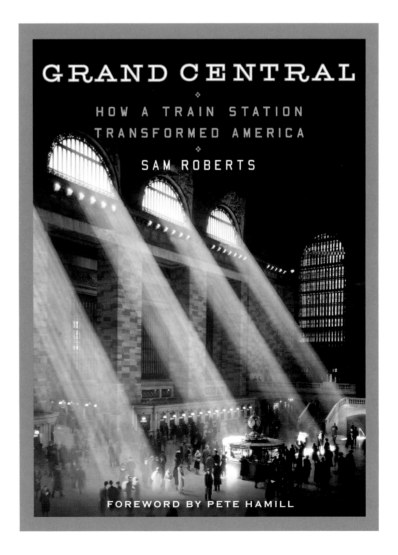

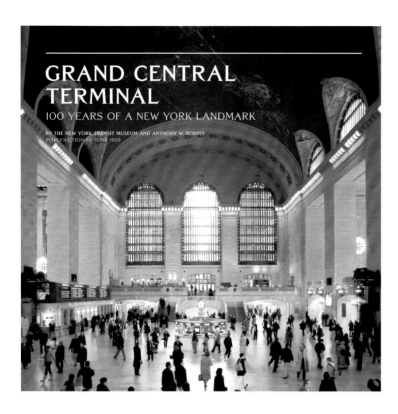

In addition to Belle's and Leighton's book, we have *Grand Central Terminal: 100 Years of a New York Landmark* by Anthony W. Robins, and *Grand Central: How a Train Station Transformed America* by Sam Roberts. Inevitably, these books overlap, though each has its distinctive point of view. Robins's *Grand Central Terminal*, produced in concert with the New York Transit Museum, has far the greater wealth of archival images. Indeed, no greater feast of such images exists between hard covers. If Belle's and Leighton's is a text illustrated with archival and contemporary images, Robins's is a picture book, in which the text comprises mainly extended captions and set-off quotations. But don't let that fool you. Robins has provided the most factually informative of these books. His is also the one among the three books to do something like justice to Jules-Félix Coutan, and, in general, to the ornamental detail of the terminal. A very nice spread of pictures and words illuminatingly compares the Park Avenue Viaduct to the Pont Alexandre III, and Robins is the only one of the authors who sees fit to tell us something about the École des Beaux-Arts and to note that Warren worked under *patrons* Honoré Daumet and Charles Girault in

Paris. I am a little troubled, though, that Condit's book, duly cited by Belle and Leighton, fails to make it into Robins's bibliography. Indeed, Robins's bibliography is also troubling for its heavy reliance on articles from the *New York Times*, with a few *New York Herald Tribune* pieces thrown in, suggesting that he made heavy use of the ProQuest database and chose to ignore other, potentially even more helpful, articles from other New York papers that are not indexed at that database. Intriguingly, Robins has little to offer on the renovation—Beyer Blinder Belle go unmentioned in his text!

Of the books, perhaps my favorite is Sam Roberts's *Grand Central*, which, if it does not quite prove the contention of its subtitle—*How a Train Station Transformed America*—nonetheless tells the terminal's story in a sprightly, engaging manner such as we would fully expect from one of New York's most esteemed city-beat journalists. And like Pete Hamill, who provides a characteristically lyrical foreword to the book, Roberts benefits from a not-too-close relationship to the world of architects and design theorists. He unaffectedly swoons over the classical beauty of the terminal, justly praises Coutan (and gets his name right), and even gives proper respect to Henry Hope Reed, noting that Jacqueline Kennedy Onassis, esteemed for her role in persuading New York officials to defend the suit brought by Penn Central and thus regarded by many as the savior of the terminal, said reading his *The Golden City* was "like finding a long-sought friend or mentor." Roberts's is a work of history and reportage, and as such is not the rich visual feast the other books are.

What remains to be written is the story of how New York became one of the great classical cities of the world, why it made perfect sense that such should be the city's destiny, and how New York made the classical new and thrillingly modern—and how Grand Central Terminal embodies and encapsulates this extraordinary story.

Francis Morrone is an architectural historian and the author of eleven books, including, with Henry Hope Reed, The New York Public Library: The Architecture and Decoration of the Stephen A. Schwarzman Building *(2011, W.W. Norton). He is the recipient of the 2012 Arthur Ross Award for History and Journalism given by the Institute of Classical Architecture & Art.*

Figure 2 (opposite): "The complex layers of the Grand Central Terminal," from a New York Central brochure, c. 1939, from *Grand Central Terminal: 100 Years of a New York Landmark,* by the New York Transit Museum and Anthony W. Robins, Stewart, Tabori & Chang, 2012. Reproduced with permission.

Section opener (pages 78-79): The "Sky Ceiling" of the Main Concourse, from *Grand Central Terminal: 100 Years of a New York Landmark* by the New York Transit Museum and Anthony W. Robins, Stewart, Tabori & Chang, 2012. Reproduced with permission.

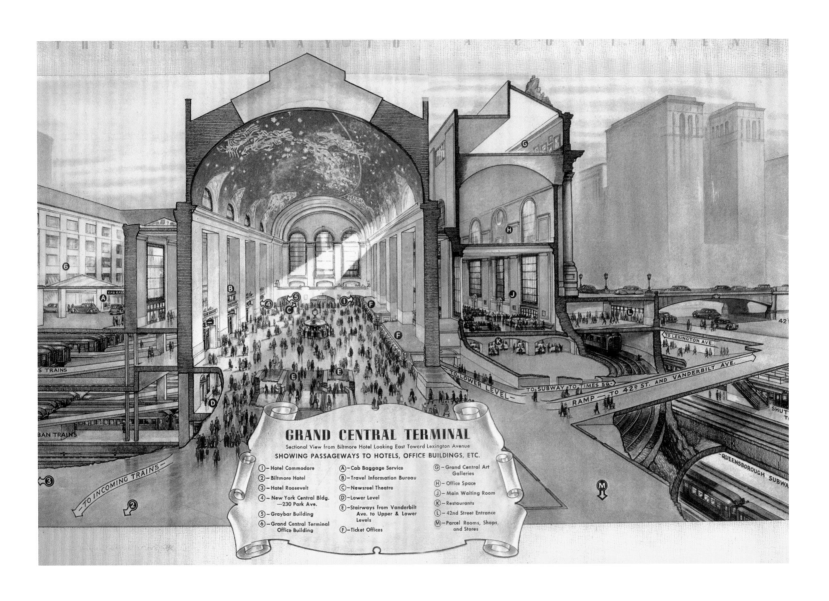

GRAND CENTRAL TERMINAL
Sectional View from Biltmore Hotel Looking East Toward Lexington Avenue
SHOWING PASSAGEWAYS TO HOTELS, OFFICE BUILDINGS, ETC.

1 — Hotel Commodore
2 — Biltmore Hotel
3 — Hotel Roosevelt
4 — New York Central Bldg. —230 Park Ave.
5 — Graybar Building
6 — Grand Central Terminal Office Building

A — Cab Baggage Service
B — Travel Information Bureau
C — Newsreel Theatre
D — Lower Level
E — Stairways from Vanderbilt Ave. to Upper & Lower Levels
F — Ticket Offices

G — Grand Central Art Galleries
H — Office Space
J — Main Waiting Room
K — Restaurants
L — 42nd Street Entrance
M — Parcel Rooms, Shops, and Stores

Administration
and Sponsors

Section opener, pages 92-93: Model of The Pantheon, Rome, in gypsum plaster with additional detail in white metal and etched brass, 22" x 18" x 15", by Timothy Richards, Bath, United Kingdom, winner of the Arthur Ross Award for Artisanship, 2013.

HENRY HOPE REED HONOR ROLL

The ICAA wishes to salute the following firms and individuals for their generous contributions in honor of Henry Hope Reed, Jr. (1915-2013). These contributions support, maintain, and improve the vital teaching assets at the Institute that include the Henry Hope Reed Classroom and non-lending research library, the historic plaster casts collection, and the Dick Reid Teaching Collection. Support was also designated to Columbia University's Avery Library, which established the Henry Hope Reed Archive, and compliments the resources and tools we use daily.

The ICAA Board of Trustees gratefully acknowledge the Arthur Ross Foundation* as the originator of a special grant and Mrs. Janet Ross for her continued support.

LATROBE
Edward Bass
Françoise and Andrew Skurman

———

PATRON
Catesby Leigh
Charlotte Moss
Electronics Design Group, Inc.
Eric J. Smith Architect, P.C.
John B. Murray Architect, LLC

———

SUSTAINERS
Emerson Adams, Mary Ballard, Shelley Belling,
Minor L. Bishop, William Bruning, David Brussat,
Linda S. Collins, Antoinette Denisof, Jean-François Gabriel,
Thomas S. Hayes, Clem Labine, James Leslie II,
Calder Loth, David Ludwig, David Morton,
Elizabeth Rogers, Karen Rubin, Steven W. Semes, Jack Taylor,
Seth Joseph Weine, Elizabeth Jones White, Edward Powis Jones,
Peter C. Jones, Hage Engineering PC, Kaese & Lynch Architecture
and Engineering, Lloyd P. Zuckerberg and Charlotte Triefus,
Newington-Cropsey Cultural Studies Center,
Premiere Custom & Decorative Painting,
Shore Point Architecture, P.A.,
The Grand Prospect Hall

———

*The Arthur Ross Foundation closed December 31, 2012

SPONSORS

The publication of *The Classicist No. 11* has been made possible thanks to the
generous contributions of the following:

E. R. Butler & Co.

———

Peter Pennoyer Architects

———

ABC Worldwide Stone Trading
Andrew Skurman Architects
Chadsworth Incorporated
Compass Ironworks
Curtis & Windham Architects, LLC
Dyad Communications, Inc.
Ferguson & Shamamian Architects, LLP
G. P. Schafer Architect, PLLC
Gregory Lombardi Design
Historical Concepts
Hyde Park Mouldings
Jan Gleysteen Architects
John B. Murray Architect, LLC
John Milner Architects
Ken Tate Architect, P.A.
Leeds Custom Design
Leonard Porter Studio, LLC
McKinnon & Harris
Reilly Windows & Doors
Robert A. M. Stern Architects, LLP
S. Donadic Inc.
Sebastian Construction Group
The Marker Group
Vella Interiors, Inc.
Waterworks

———

Flower Construction
Horizon Builders
Griffiths Construction Inc.
Miller & Wright Architects

———

Historic Doors, LLC
Jeff Allen Landscape Architecture, LLC
Sanchez & Maddux, Inc.
Traditional Cut Stone

———

Cathy Kincaid Interiors
Duncan G. Stroik Architect, Inc.
Hart Howarton
Jackson & Ryan Architects, Inc.
James Leslie Design Assoc., Inc.
Lowe Hardware
Lucas/Eilers Desgn Associates, LLP
Molly Isaksen Interiors
Saienni Stairs, LLC
Shore Point Architecture, P.A.

———

MARBLE
GRANITE

SANDSTONE
QUARTZITE

LIMESTONE
TRAVERTINE

ARTISAN MOSAIC
SEMI-PRECIOUS

EXTERIOR
LANDSCAPE STONE

FRENCH FLOORING
ENGINEERED-STONE

CHADSWORTH INCORPORATED

COLUMNS • BALUSTRADES • PERGOLAS • MILLWORK • SHUTTERS

800.486.2118 | FAX: 910.763.3191

www.COLUMNS.com

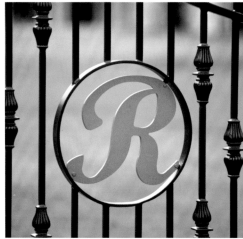

CURTIS & WINDHAM
Architects
INCORPORATED

WWW.CURTISANDWINDHAM.COM

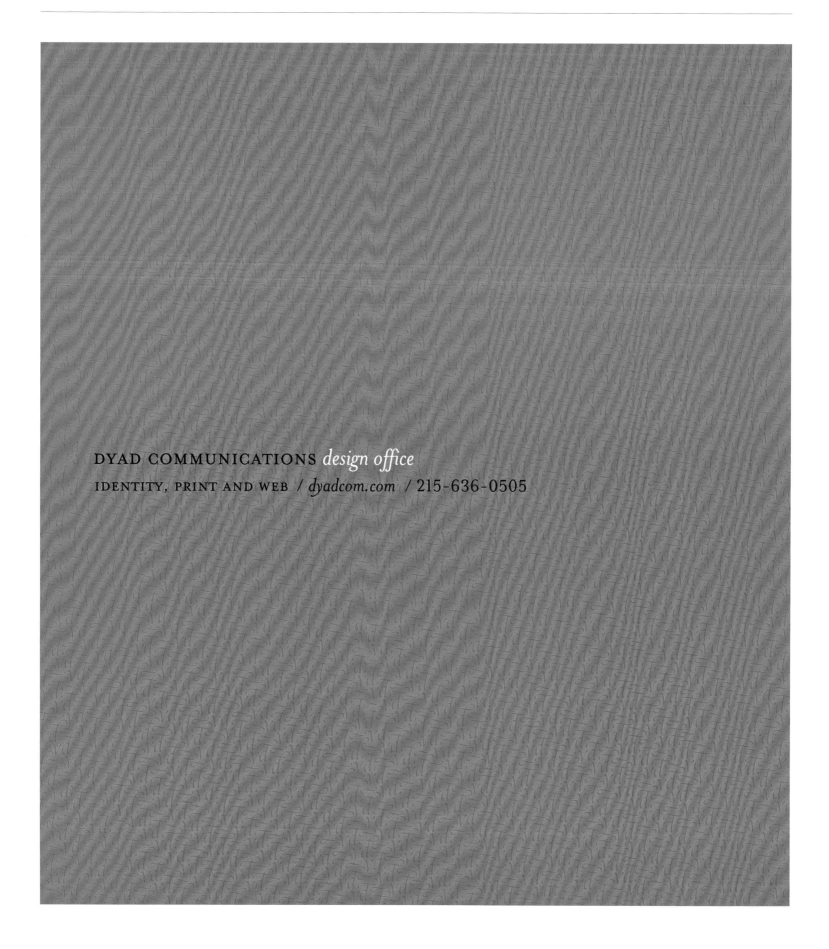

DYAD COMMUNICATIONS *design office*

IDENTITY, PRINT AND WEB / *dyadcom.com* / 215-636-0505

B̈

E.R. BUTLER & CO.

The W.C. Vaughan Company Collection

E.R. BUTLER & CO. is pleased to offer the W.C. Vaughan Co.'s complete line of Early American and Georgian period hardware. For over a century, the W.C. Vaughan Co. manufactured high quality architectural, builders' and furniture hardware from its unique design archive, a collection of early nineteenth-century hardware patterns and drawings from houses throughout New England and the Atlantic seaboard.

Renowned for its expertise, the W.C. Vaughan Co. always relied upon the most precise tooling and best manufacturing methods available, supplying hardware for such restoration projects as Colonial Williamsburg. As W.C. Vaughan's successor, E.R. Butler & Co. continues to produce hardware of superior design, workmanship and finish so that the reproduction conveys the distinct qualities of the original.

Early American and Georgian period door knobs range in size from 3 inch diameter centre knobs to 1 ⅝ inch diameter screen door knobs. Cabinet and fine furniture knobs range in size from 1 ½ inch diameter cabinet knobs to ¾ inch diameter drawer knobs. Available in many decorative finishes, all design series are fully complimented by architectural trim including hinges, locks, cane bolts, cylinder rings and covers, key escutcheons and covers, thumb turns, doorstops, etc.

"OG" SERIES
DESIGN SCALE

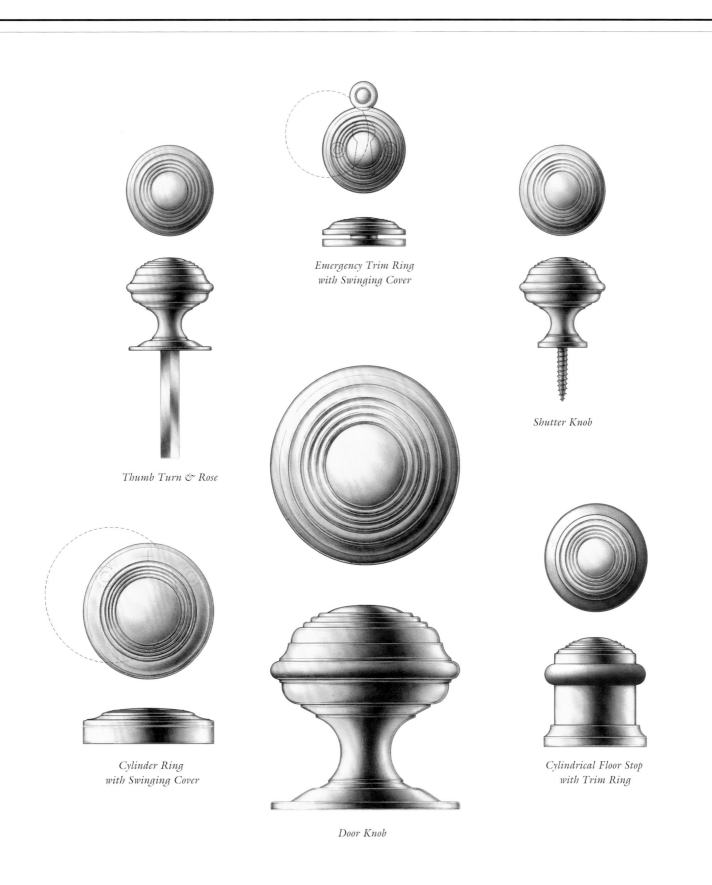

*Emergency Trim Ring
with Swinging Cover*

Shutter Knob

Thumb Turn & Rose

*Cylinder Ring
with Swinging Cover*

*Cylindrical Floor Stop
with Trim Ring*

Door Knob

"OG" SERIES
DESIGN SUITE

B̈

E. R. Butler & Co.

MANUFACTURERS

WWW.ERBUTLER.COM

CATALOGUES AVAILABLE TO THE TRADE

SHOWROOMS BY APPOINTMENT ONLY

TECHNICAL DRAWING: JOHN SYKES FETTERMAN   RENDERING: MARGITTA ZACHERT   TYPOGRAPHY: JOHN PACKER

FERGUSON &
SHAMAMIAN
ARCHITECTS, LLP

270 LAFAYETTE STREET, NEW YORK, NY 10012
TELEPHONE: 212-941-8088
www.fergusonshamamian.com

Photo: Michael Mundy

G. P. Schafer Architect, PLLC

—— ARCHITECTURE & DESIGN ——

WWW.GPSCHAFER.COM

GREGORY LOMBARDI DESIGN

Landscape Architecture

Cambridge · Chatham · Palm Beach | 617.492.2808 www.lombardidesign.com

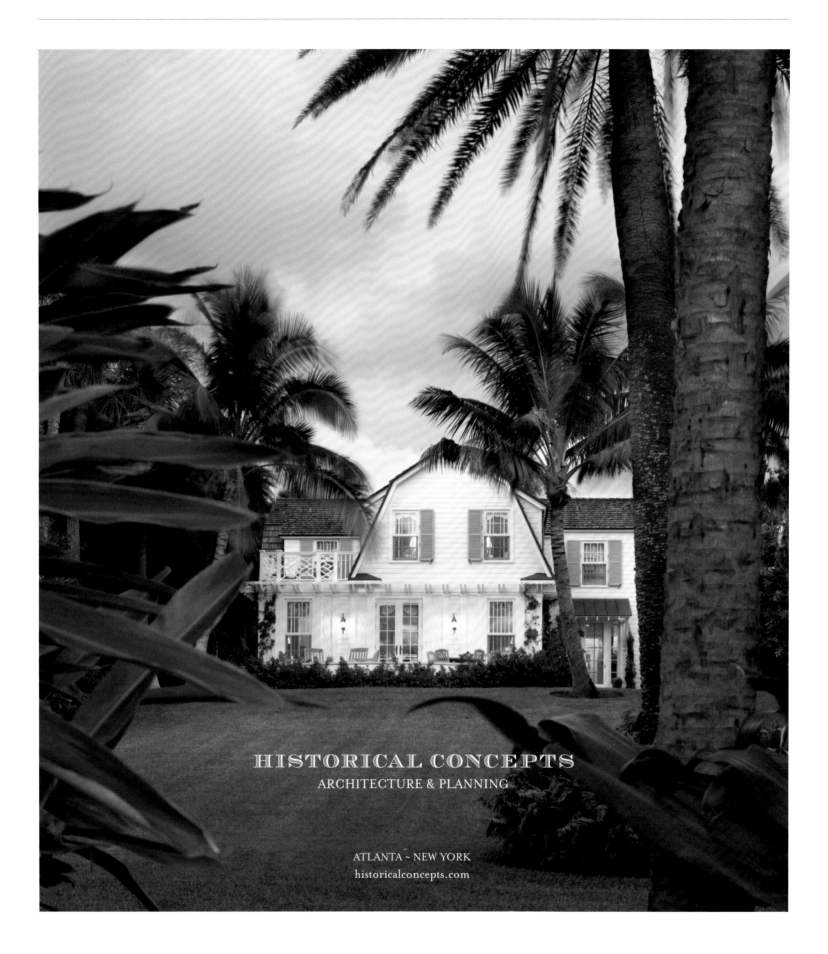

HISTORICAL CONCEPTS
ARCHITECTURE & PLANNING

ATLANTA ~ NEW YORK
historicalconcepts.com

HYDE PARK MOULDINGS
WWW.HYDE-PARK.COM

JAN GLEYSTEEN ARCHITECTS
Wellesley, Massachusetts • www.JanGleysteenInc.com

JOHN B. MURRAY ARCHITECT

48 West 37th Street, 10th Floor, New York, New York

212•242•8600

JBMARCHITECT.COM

Restoration of the Nemours Mansion & Gardens, Wilmington, DE

New Children's Cottage in a Garden

JOHN MILNER ARCHITECTS
DESIGN & PRESERVATION

Chadds Ford, Pennsylvania

www.johnmilnerarchitects.com

KENTATE

ARCHITECT

433 N. Columbia Street, Suite 2 Covington, LA 70433   985.845.8181 *kentatearchitect.com*

Drawing courtesy of
Domiane Forte.

Supporting Architects and Artists
through the ICAA.

LEEDS
CUSTOM DESIGN

435 Southern Blvd.   West Palm Beach, FL   33405   561.659.3134

·LEONARD·PORTER·STVDIO·

PAINTINGS OF ANTIQVITY AND CLASSICAL MYTHOLOGY

WWW·LEONARDPORTER·COM

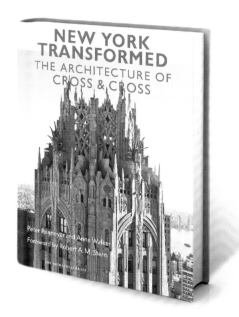

"How wise [Pennoyer and Walker] are to write about this firm; architects of many buildings in and around New York that are admired even though the names of their designers are virtually forgotten."
— ROBERT A.M. STERN, *FROM THE FOREWORD*

IN 1907, NEW YORK CITY existed mainly as a low-rise metropolis, but with unbridled wealth pouring in, the Manhattan of the future was starting to take shape. Critical in the city's transformation were architect John Walter Cross and his younger brother and partner, Eliot Cross. And yet, the names Cross and Cross have been largely forgotten until now.

In *NEW YORK TRANSFORMED: The Architecture of Cross & Cross,* architect Peter Pennoyer and historian Anne Walker trace the exceptional 35-year tenure of these two brothers, exploring their work—including their iconic RCA Victor building on Lexington Avenue and their building for Tiffany & Co. on Fifth Avenue—as well as their innovative real estate enterprise, Webb & Knapp, that allowed the brothers to create opportunities for profit in their projects and forever changed the real estate industry. Featuring more than 300 historic and modern photographs, as well as architectural plans and sketches of their projects—including estates for Electra Havemeyer Webb, founder of the Shelburne Museum, and Henry Francis du Pont, founder of the Winterthur Museum—*NEW YORK TRANSFORMED* showcases how the brothers and businessmen transformed pockets of Manhattan and beyond with their nuanced taste.

New York Transformed: The Architecture of Cross & Cross by Peter Pennoyer and Anne Walker
Monacelli | ISBN: 978-1580933803 | $60.00 US | March 18, 2014 | Hardcover | 240 pages | 300 photos

PETER PENNOYER ARCHITECTS
PPAPC.COM

HOUSE IN MILLBROOK, NEW YORK
Peter Pennoyer Architects, 2013

McKINNON AND HARRIS®

ESTATE · GARDEN · YACHT FURNITURE

www.mckinnonharris.com

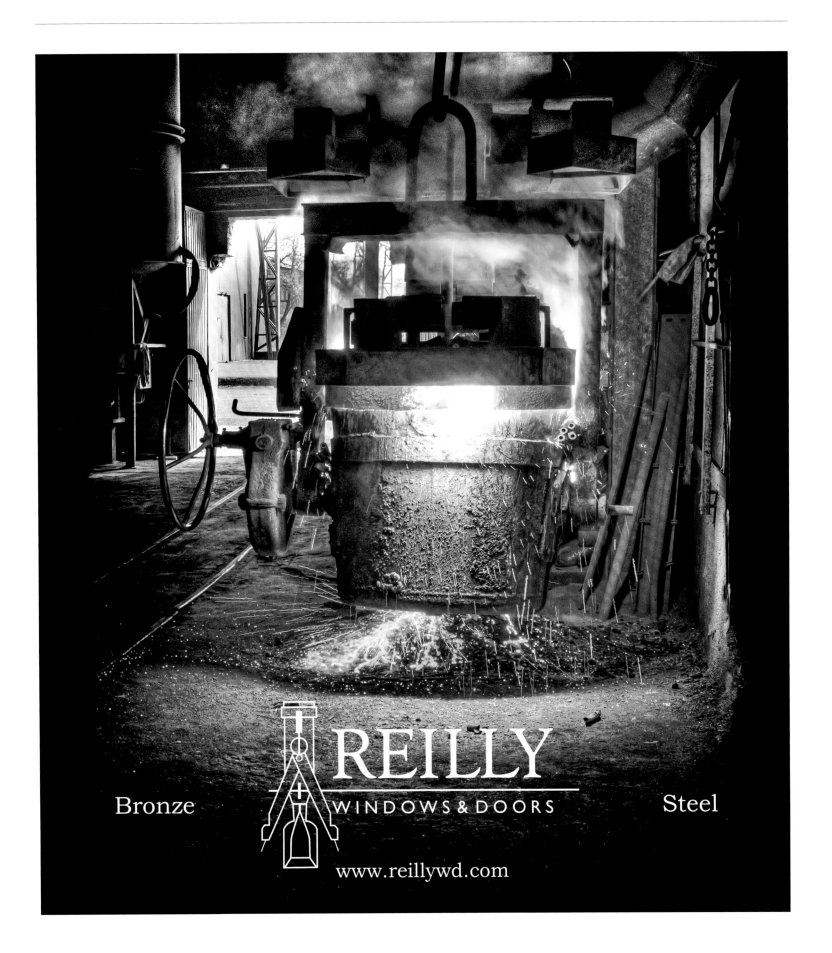

Bronze · REILLY · WINDOWS & DOORS · Steel

www.reillywd.com

RAMSA
ROBERT A.M. STERN ARCHITECTS

GEORGE W. BUSH PRESIDENTIAL LIBRARY AND MUSEUM

460 WEST 34TH STREET   NEW YORK, NEW YORK 10001   TEL 212 967 5100   www.ramsa.com

S.DONADICINC
CONSTRUCTION MANAGEMENT

45-25 39TH STREET LONG ISLAND CITY NY 11104   WWW.DONADIC.COM

SEBASTIAN
Construction Group

BUILDING TRULY EXCEPTIONAL
RESIDENCES SINCE 1948

www.SEBASTIANCG.com

DALLAS | HOUSTON

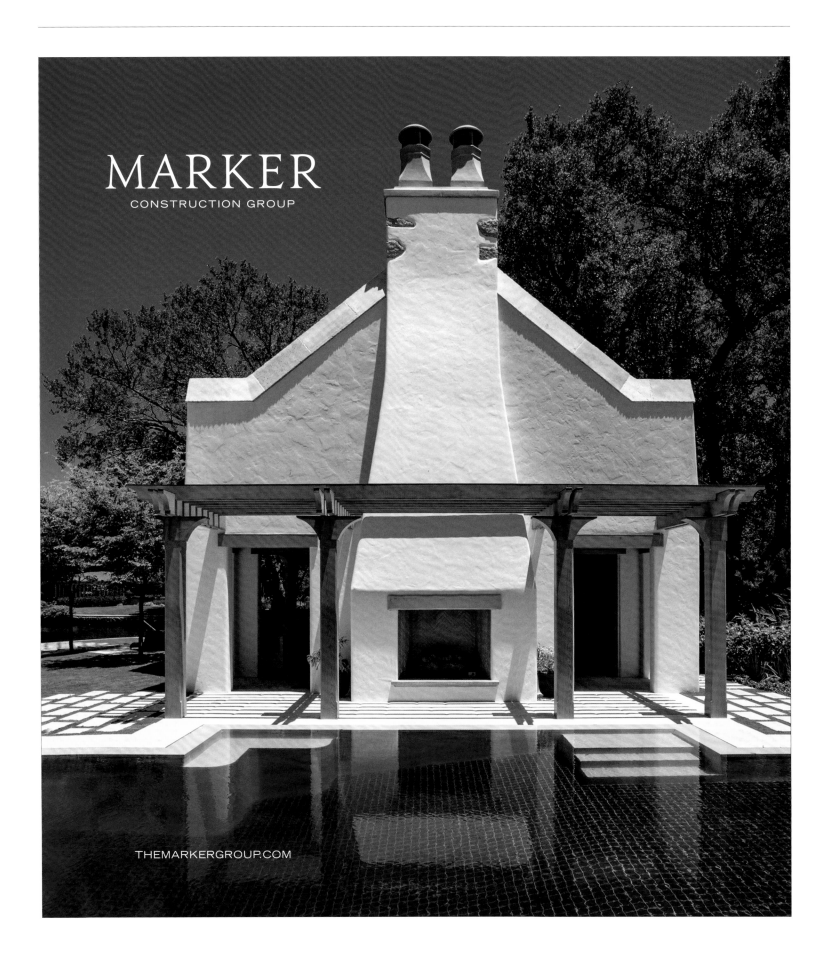

MARKER
CONSTRUCTION GROUP

THEMARKERGROUP.COM

DISTRICT TILE IS A TRADEMARK OF WATERWORKS IP CO. LLC.

ESTB. 1978

WATERWORKS

**UNIQUELY STRIKING SURFACES,
FITTINGS, FIXTURES AND ACCESSORIES**

WWW.WATERWORKS.COM

 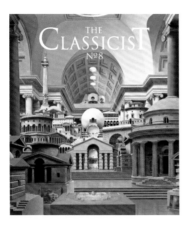 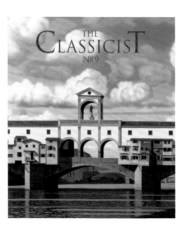 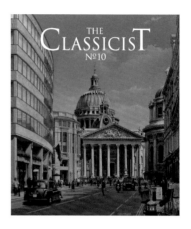

THE CLASSICIST ANNOUNCES A CALL FOR PAPERS AND PROJECTS

SCHOLARS, PROFESSIONALS, AND STUDENTS are invited to submit proposals for academic articles, professional projects, or student work that might be suitable for publication in upcoming issues of *The Classicist.* We are actively seeking:

ACADEMIC ARTICLES, which will be subject to a double-blind peer-review process and may treat any subject related to classical architecture, urbanism, or decorative arts, historical or contemporary, relating to either theory or practice;

PROFESSIONAL WORK for architectural, urban, or landscape design in the classical tradition, whether completed or not and including competition entries, ideally produced within the last eighteen months;

ARTWORKS in any medium executed in architectural settings or otherwise representing the alliance between architecture and allied arts in the classical tradition;

STUDENT PROJECTS that explore similar themes.

We wish to present in the pages of *The Classicist* a broad sample of research and work in the field, diverse in subject matter, character, and geographical origin, and we particularly invite material from students and younger scholars and professionals.

Abstracts for academic articles may be submitted at any time, accompanied by a cover letter including full contact information.

Those whose abstracts are accepted will be notified regarding deadlines for submission of completed articles and requirements for graphic materials. Proposals deemed suitable may also be considered for future issues at the discretion of the Editor. Abstracts should be sent, along with completed checklist and application, to *journal@classicist.org.*

Those wishing to propose professional or student projects may submit up to three examples of recent work (ideally from the past 2 years). Among the professional projects, although preference will be given to completed buildings, unrealized projects and competition entries are welcome. Send a brief description (maximum 500 words) of each project, including date of completion and a list of participating team members, with up to four digital images per project for preliminary review (jpegs are preferred no larger than 500 KB). Projects are subject to review by the Editor and a review committee named by the ICAA Publications Committee. Student and professional project submittals, along with completed checklist and application, must be submitted to *journal@classicist.org.* Images for selected projects will require publishable formatting and applicants will be notified with specifications and deadlines for final submittal of materials.

For information on past editions, visit *The Classicist* section of our website: *classicist.org/publications-and-bookshop/the-classicist.*

COLOPHON

❦

Production:
Composed with Quark XPress 9.5 and Mac OS X

Text: Korean Neo Matte Art 157gsm
Cover: Chinese Butterfly C2S 230gsm
Separations: 300 Line Screen
Printing: Offset Lithography
Binding: Perfect Bound
Edition: 2,500

Typefaces:
Centaur, designed by Bruce Rogers
for The Metropolitan Museum of Art in 1912–14,
based on the Roman type cut in Venice by Nicolas Jensen in 1469,
modified by Dyad Communications.

Trajan, designed by Carol Twombly in 1988,
based on the inscription carved on the pedestal of
Trajan's Column, Rome 113 A.D.

❦